AMERICAN
PATCHWORK

AMERICAN PATCHWORK

True Stories from Quilters

- - - - - - - - - - - - - - - - - -

EDITED BY

Sonja Hakala

Thomas Dunne Books

ST. MARTIN'S PRESS ⚜ NEW YORK

Copyright acknowledgments appear on page 229.

Design by Maggie Goodman

ISBN-13: 978-0-312-34788-8
ISBN-10: 0-312-34788-X

First Edition: April 2007

10   9   8   7   6   5   4   3   2   1

For Jay,

always for Jay

CONTENTS

= = = = =

ACKNOWLEDGMENTS

- - - - -

This is the place where I get to say thank you to all of the people who have helped, encouraged, supported, advised, or cheered from the sidelines while *American Patchwork* came into being. I just hope I don't forget anybody and if I do, please forgive me!

First of all, I want to take a deep and grateful bow in the direction of all of the contributors to this book. I'm not sure my *Webster's Collegiate Dictionary* has words that are adequate to express my thanks for your willingness to share such poignant, personal, funny, interesting, and touching tales with someone you really didn't know. Your trust has often made me feel humble. I can only describe working with all of you as being at the best quilter's guild meeting you can imagine. Your warm companionship has made the journey from idea to book a real pleasure.

Thank you.

Thanks to my friend Sue Wheeler, who introduced me to that magical tool called the rotary cutter and sparked my enthusiasm for quilting with her own. To Lauren Sherman, Kristin Burch, Nellie Pennington, Lindas Roghaar and Shemanske, Sam Ankerson, my Aunt Fluff Kennedy, and my sister Heidi Trottier, whose enthusiasm for *American Patchwork* encouraged quilters with stories to tell to write them down and send them to me. To all my friends, family, and the staff at my local quilt shops who loaned me books, answered my questions, sent me articles, told me about quilt shows and shops, or just otherwise alerted me to anything about quilting that they thought would interest me. To the staff at the Howe Library in Hanover, New Hampshire, who gave me access to the women who made the magnificent quilts displayed in the library before it was renovated. (I hope they come back!)

To my agent and friend, Linda Roghaar, whose love of craft inspired the idea for *American Patchwork* and whose enthusiastic support of this book made it possible.

To Anne Merrow, my editor at St. Martin's Press, whose sure hand is reassuring.

To my son, Jesse, who's the best cheerleader a mom could ask for.

And most of all, the hugest thank-you to my husband, Jay Davis, for labeling, stamping, folding, encouraging, making cups of tea, cooking supper, making trips to the post office, listening, suggesting, encouraging, rubbing sore shoulders, and just generally being the best all-around guy in the world.

Sonja Hakala
West Hartford, Vermont

It took me more than twenty years, nearly twenty-five, I reckon, in the evenings after supper when the children were all put to bed. My whole life is in that quilt. It scares me sometimes when I look at it. All my joys and all my sorrows are stitched into those little pieces. When I was proud of the boys and when I was downright provoked and angry with them. When the girls annoyed me or when they gave me warm feelings around my heart. And John, too. He was stitched into that quilt and all the thirty years we were married. Sometimes I loved him and sometimes I sat there hating him as I pieced the patches together. So they are all in that quilt, my hopes and fears, my joys and sorrows, my loves and hates. I tremble sometimes when I remember what that quilt knows about me.

—MARGARITE ICKIS,
quoting her great-grandmother in
Anonymous Was a Woman by Mirra Bank

INTRODUCTION

- - - - -

It had been gray for days, the thickening gloom of November in Vermont. Outside, a sharp wind hurled sheets of cold rain against the sides of a small farmhouse, but in the kitchen fire licked up the sides of logs piled on the hearth. Every once in a while, the burning logs shifted their positions, crumbling into embers that pulsed red and orange as they gave up their heat.

A woman sat in a chair pulled close to the warming blaze, struggling to see her needle and thread in the low light given off by the fire and a tallow candle on the table at her elbow. Suddenly Jane Stickle sat up straight, her heart quickening just a little. At age forty-six, the cares of farming the rocky fields of northern New England showed in her face. Her hair, now graying, crouched in a knot at the back of her neck. But as she reached for her small pair of scissors, Jane's eyes glowed. She'd finished it, the quilt.

She gathered it up in her lap, running her fingers over the 5,602 pieces of fabric that she'd cut and stitched together in 225 patterns, each one different from all the others. Her fingers lingered over one of the corner squares where she'd stitched her name, Jane A. Stickle, and the words "in war-time 1863."

The country had been at war for two years, a terrifying dance of death between those who called themselves the Union and those who preferred the name Confederacy. Vermont had enshrined the idea of abolition in its constitution so Union feeling ran high in the Green Mountain State. It's probable that Jane

Stickle knew some of the 32,000 men who marched off to war from Vermont. Perhaps she'd loved one of the 6,000 men who never came back. If she did, she left no record of it.

It gets very cold in Vermont in the winter and the need for warm blankets at night is keen. But there are easier and quicker ways to provide covers for a bed than the way Jane Stickle chose. So why did she spend hours and hours piecing together patches of fabric, many no bigger than her thumb, to make a blanket?

In part, common beliefs about the origins of quilting in America lie more in the region of legend than truth. If asked, most folks say that quilting developed when frugal colonial-era women, eager to make cloth stretch as far as they could, saved scraps of fabric and sewed them together to make quilts. But that's not quite accurate.

The process of quilting has been practiced in many places and in many times around the world. At its most basic, a quilt consists of two layers of fabric filled in the middle with an insulating material, such as wool or cotton. In order to keep the insulation in place, a quiltmaker makes stitches through the top and bottom layers (and the filling) across the length and width of the fabric. Quilts have been used in petticoats and as protection between a knight's skin and his armor.

When European women first arrived in North America, they brought their needles and thread with them. But the mere work required for survival—gardening, food preparation and preservation, sewing clothes, providing heat for the home, and cleaning—left no time for making blankets that required small pieces of fabric sewed together.

The first quilts in America were of the type that's now called "whole cloth." Typically, these are two single pieces of fabric—often imprinted with large, ornate designs called "medallions"—that are stitched together and sandwiched with a layer of batting in between. Remember, this was a time when cloth was manu-factures by handworked looms: it was not plentiful and women valued it too much to cut it up.

Three events combined to create the circumstances that gave birth to what we now call the "patchwork quilt." First of all, the Industrial Revolution took textile manufacturing away from hand-powered looms and put it into factories, starting in the 1820s, so that more people had access to more fabric than ever before in human history. As it progressed, this industrialization took away many of the trades that women had practiced along-side men during the early settling of the country. By 1850, a woman's "place" had become the home and avenues for work and creative expression were narrowed to the domestic sphere. And finally, Elias Howe patented the first sewing machine with an eye-pointed needle on September 10, 1846. This meant that sewing clothes was easier and quicker than ever because stitching was faster and more precise. And when you make clothes, you get scraps of fabric.

But all this utilitarian background alone does not explain the origin of the patchwork quilt. If all you want is a frugal way to make a bed covering by using up scrap, why cut fabric leftovers into precise shapes and arrange them in pleasing patterns of color? In other words, what is it that made Jane Stickle quilt?

I think it could be successfully argued that, in the United States, more people express their creativity through the art of quilting than through any other single medium—more than wa-tercolors, more than words, more than marble or clay, more than yarn (which I would bet is a close second). Every day, mil-lions of women, and some men, express their inborn desire for beauty in fabric, needle, and thread. Quilting is as much an ex-pression of the human yearning to reach beyond this life as a novel or a cave painting, and for many people, it's more accessible.

That's why I think Jane Stickle quilted, to express the sorrow and fear she felt watching her country tear itself apart, to feel the soothing power of creating beauty, to satisfy a yearning for immortality.

But quilting is more than a desire for beauty made manifest in cloth. As all the writers in *American Patchwork* will tell you, quilting can be an act of will, of self-expression, and of love. Quilting keeps the hand and mind busy so that the heart can heal when there's trouble, which is as good a definition of therapy as you'll ever find. It sparks imagination through color, pattern, and possibility. It creates powerful relationships among the people who practice it. And every quilt is as individual as our fingerprints.

That's an awful lot to expect from a few scraps of cloth, isn't it? But the quilters and quilt lovers you're going to meet will convince you that it's all true. They'll make you laugh, they'll make you think, they're going to touch your heart.

So put away the rotary cutter, pick the threads off your sleeve, and join us in a celebration of quilts, quilters, and their stories. The fat quarters can wait for just a little while.

—Sonja Hakala

P.S. Jane Stickle's quilt goes on display at the Bennington Museum in Bennington, Vermont, from early September to mid-October every year. It's the Great-Grandmother of patchwork quilts, and if you ever get the chance to see it, do so. It's just amazing.

AMERICAN
PATCHWORK

CIRCLES IN TIME

- - - - -

SHARONA FISCHRUP

One long line of fabric, that's how my life story is told.

It seems like a long time ago, when the quilting bug hit me. My first quilt was made in Jerusalem, from velvets bought at a tailor shop in the heart of the city. It was a baby quilt for my friend Aviva's fifth child—a beautiful daughter—back in 1976.

When I moved to San Francisco, I made friends with a woman named Diana, a woman who had been bit hard by the quilting bug. She roped me in through friendship and our mutual love of fabric. She took me to a store called New Pieces, in Berkeley, on one of my favorite shopping streets, Solano Avenue.

Carlberg was the owner then. The store had a wooden stage in back for Friday night concerts. During the week, a harpsichord sat on the stage. The store's name was a play on music and on his partner Judiyaba's quilting. This was in the eighties, 1985 or '86. My daughter was just a few years old.

I remember signing up for a class at New Pieces with Lucy Hilty, a hand quilting class. What a treat. She was a little English woman, round, petite, sweet, and *smart*. She had us doing the math to get our borders turned out just right so that the pattern flowed. I loved it.

After taking her class I designed a quilt with a smiling fish in the center, a circular border of feathers, and then another circular

feather border. On the paper drawing, it all came together perfectly thanks to Lucy's math lessons.

It was another few years before I started to work on that quilt.
Okay, maybe more than a few years. It was 1992 and I took it
along with me when my daughter and I traveled to Surfer's Par-
adise in Queensland, Australia, to see Aviva, the good friend whose
daughter had received my first quilt. I did a lot of stitching on that
trip. I was so pleased to be finally working on it. The plane ride
was long and the quilting kept me busy while my daughter, who
was eight at the time, slept.

I finished the quilt in time to show it in my guild's biannual
show, Voices in Cloth. My teacher, Lucy, loved it, and I was so
proud to have it up there for all to see. At my friend Aviva's sugges-
tion, I'd put beads on it—very revolutionary for me—representing
air bubbles coming from the fish.

Time passed. I was an active East Bay Heritage Quilters guild
member by then, even serving on its board of directors. I retired
from my day job when my daughter was in seventh grade to become a full-time mom and quilter. But after several years of retirement, I got itchy to "do something" and took a class on how
to find the perfect job. After a few months of "back to work"
training and putting together a résumé that suited me, I applied
at my local quilt shop, New Pieces, now owned by Sally Davey.
Something that Sally told me during that interview stuck. She
told me I'd never be a customer again, I'd be forever pegged as a
New Pieces employee, always there to help others.

After working for more than thirty years in Corporate America, in the computer industry, I thought I had died and gone to
heaven in my new job. I had always been a seamstress but I made
my living in computers. Now I was selling fabric to quilters—who
loved sewing as much as I did. I still can't get over how lucky I was
to have gotten that job.

I studied with more and more teachers, got a photograph of one of my quilts published in a book of Gai Perry's, got accepted in the Pacific International Quilt Festival, got more active in East Bay Heritage Quilters, and really started expressing my inner self in my quilts. In other words, I generally enjoyed all there is to enjoy as a collector of fabric and a quilter.

Years passed—three or four, I don't know how many—and I was as happy working at New Pieces as I had been on my first day there. My daughter, Leila, was growing. The teen years were trying but I had my community of quilters and my work at New Pieces.

My brother passed away the week before September 11, 2001, and I expressed my grief in a quilt that was published in *America from the Heart* by Karey Bresnahan. Then, when my daughter graduated and moved on with her own life, Sally decided to sell New Pieces. My dear husband, Jack, and I looked over the prospect of buying the business but decided against it. Another quilt or two passed through my fingers and then Sally talked about closing the store.

Well, that decided it. New Pieces and the community of quilters it serves was more important than anything else. I had to buy—so we did.

New Pieces became formally owned by Jack and me on January 1, 2004. When I remember that class I took with Lucy Hilty back in 1985, it seems impossible that I would own this very same shop. It continues to be a gathering place for quilters and teachers from all over the world.

Recently, while at Asilomar with my guild, I finished my daughter's high school graduation quilt—two and a half years in the making and hand quilted free-form à la Joe Cunningham—and I was moved to tears. I felt like I had just run the seven and a half miles of the Bay-to-Breakers race and finished! The folks in the room cried with me because they knew what it meant to complete such an undertaking. There's a piece of woven Japanese fabric on the back of it that cost way more than I normally spend on any fabric. I bought it from Sally Davey when she owned New Pieces. The main piece of fabric on the quilt's top is a creme sateen that I bought from Carlberg when I took that first class from Lucy Hilty.

Now my friend Aviva and my teacher Lucy have passed on, Carlberg and Sally have moved on, and Leila has grown. Yet we are still together through our fabrics, a long line of fabric touching and connecting us all.

SHARONA FISCHRUP *lives with her dear hubby, Jack, and their vizsla, Mowgli, in the East Bay area of Northern California. She lives for her daughter, Leila, her mom, JoAnn, and her wonderful family and friends. She also lives for her quilting community—all the folks who share her passion. She thanks Jaye Lapachet for telling her about* American Patchwork *so she could tell this story. Visit Sharona in person at New Pieces or at www.newpieces.com.*

A GUY THAT SEWS

- - - - -

JOE ZELLNER, JR.

 "You can't do that!"

"Why not?"

"Because it won't work out."

"Yes, it will."

"No. Also, you can't cut it that way."

"Why not?"

"Because it won't work."

"Yes, it will."

"Fine. Do it your way."

Snip, snip. "Mom? What do I do next?"

That is how my Christmas was this year. After traveling to get together with family for the holidays, we had some time to work on projects. As a fairly new quilter, I didn't know the ropes. But as a "Guy That Sews," I knew I could do anything.

I started sewing young when my mom was making and re-pairing clothes for us kids. When she was busy working, I would do my own repairs. I enjoyed doing anything with my hands and Mom was glad to have me help out because it kept me busy and out of trouble.

After getting married, life got too hectic to think about much and after not sewing for a long time, I picked it up again as a way to keep myself sane. I mean, what else can you do when your snowmobile doesn't start, there's four feet of snow on the ground, your ice auger blades are dull, and it's thirty below?

So I started finishing my wife's projects. She'd start stuff and then get bored and put it away. I'd find them later and finish them. So I guess you could say that my love of sewing started up again because of my wife.

Making my own hunting clothes was fun. I wanted certain features on my outfit that no one was doing so I'd design my own stuff. Then came presents—gloves for the kids, bathrobes for the women of the family, hunting clothes for the guys.

Our family and our friends' families started growing up. Now there were all these babies! So what do you make a newborn? Well, it just seemed natural to make a quilt for a baby. Hence the argument at Christmas about the quilt I was trying to make.

You see, my mom has made so many quilts, she seems to do them in her sleep. And here I was, doing them on the bias and cutting all these weird angles. And when she told me that I couldn't do them that way, it just made me pigheaded. To me, as a carpenter, nothing is impossible. The stranger it is, the more I enjoy it.

Well, after a lot of frustrating moments, my first quilt turned out okay and they just keep getting better and better. Some day, I'll get back to designing and making clothes. But for now, I'm sticking to flat cloth.

"Mom? Why won't this stupid thing come out right? The points are all crooked."

JOE ZELLNER, JR., *is a carpenter who lives in the woods in northern Minnesota. He began quilting several years ago to pass the time during the long winter nights. Construction and creativity are passions of his whether they are with wood or fabric. He owes his love of sewing to his mother, who is an accomplished quilter and seamstress.*

MISS BECK'S GIFT

- - - - -

HENRY JOYCE

I think I must have one of the best jobs in the world. I'm the chief curator of the Shelburne Museum in Shelburne, Vermont, and in that capacity, I have the opportunity to interact with one of the best quilt collections you will find anywhere. The museum's founder, Electra Havemeyer Webb, was an eclectic collector who is credited with being one of the first people who, at the turn of the twentieth century, appreciated quilts as works of art. It used to be that if a quilt was displayed in a museum at all, it was merely decoration for a piece of furniture. But Mrs. Webb insisted that quilts be displayed on their own and hung so that viewers could see and appreciate their colors and patterns as well as the extraordinary talents of the women who crafted them.

Before I moved up to Vermont, my work as a curator focused on the fine arts and I had little experience with quilts. Because of that, I looked at quilts with an eye trained by painting. Consequently, I was attracted to quilts with color that really pops, like an Amish quilt we have from Lancaster County called *Concentric Squares*. Its slate blue and red squares are nested inside one another and it reminds me of Op Art paintings of the 1960s, because your eyes just can't stay still when you look at it.

My other favorites are among the Album quilts, especially a centennial quilt made by Minnie Burdick in 1876. There are thirty-six blocks in this quilt and each one of them is an original drawing in fabric. There are two scenes from the 1876 Centennial Exposition in Philadelphia, interpretations of Biblical stories such as Noah and the ark, twins in a cradle, bounty from the sea featuring lobster and crab, fruits and flowers, all sorts of animals, and scenes from her hometown of North Adams, Massachusetts. It is simultaneously sophisticated and childlike and completely original.

I'm telling you all of this so that perhaps you'll understand why I was so lukewarm about this quilt that the museum received from a quilter named Ida W. Beck back in 1955. Compared to the zing of the Amish quilts or the originality of pieces like Minnie Burdick's Album quilt, Miss Beck's gift to the museum seemed too subtle to me.

Miss Beck was born in Easton, Pennsylvania, in 1880, and because of health problems, she was a shut-in all her life. There weren't too many outlets for a woman's creativity back then except needlework, so Miss Beck devoted her life to fine embroidery, especially monogramming.

I daresay that the quilt she gave to the museum is probably the best work she ever did. It's 94 × 90 inches of quilted and embroidered cotton. The background is cream colored, and on this canvas, Miss Beck embroidered eight different versions of the alphabet, each one in a different type of lettering, with a large alphabet monogram in the center panel. There's a tree of life centered on the bottom edge that's decorated with an alphabet and flanked by interpretations of the four seasons. This incredible array of embroidering prowess is framed by a scalloped edging of soft pinks, blues, yellows, and lavenders that in turn is framed by dark green fabric attached with a feathered edge. There are six scallops on each side—twelve in all—and each one presents the name of one of the months of the year decorated by appropriate flowers.

As I said, it is extraordinary, but it just didn't have the same appeal to me as others in the collection. That's why when I put together an exhibit of 100 Masterpiece Quilts, Miss Beck's piece did not make my first cut.

But a funny thing happened on the way to hanging the exhibit. We have a building dedicated to quilts on the museum grounds, and before the Shelburne opened for the season that May, we were quite busy putting these fabric masterpieces on display, hanging each so that it would be seen to its best advantage. Somehow, when we were all done, I ended up with this gap in the exhibit. With opening day so close at hand, I didn't have time to reconfigure the exhibit or make any adjustments. It was easier to add a quilt and I thought that Miss Beck's gift would fill up the spot nicely.

Here at the Shelburne, we always try to include an educational component in our special exhibits because we've found that our visitors have so many questions about our collections of dolls, witch balls, hatboxes, tools, carriages, carousel figures, weather vanes, glass canes, and antiques. So long before the 100 Masterpiece Quilts exhibit opened, I'd contacted the Champlain Valley Quilt Guild to ask if any of the members would be willing to appear regularly at the Shelburne and bring whatever they were working on. That way, visitors could see how quilts are made and the guild members could answer questions.

The quilters also acted as guides, showing off the masterpieces in the exhibit. It wasn't long before I heard back from them that people loved all the quilts but the favorite one of all was, you guessed it, Miss Beck's. People would "ooh" over the Amish quilts and "aah" over the Album quilts, but the sound that accompanied the sight of all that embroidery and exquisite quilting was one of undeniable appreciation. It just goes to show that curators don't know everything.

So, I've learned to look twice at the individual pieces in our quilt collection and nurture an even greater interpretation of the many talents and skills of their makers, especially Miss Beck.

HENRY JOYCE *was the chief curator of the Shelburne Museum in Shelburne, Vermont. He's the author of several books about the museum's many collections, ranging from Impressionist paintings to decorative hatboxes and everything in between. You can find out more about the Shelburne on its Web site, www.shelburnemuseum.org.*

THE STORYTELLER'S DREAM

- - - - -

CATHY CARDWELL

Every quilt has its own share of memories, some funny, some very personal, some just downright eerie. While each of my quilts prompts its share of these memories, there's one in particular that's a storyteller's dream. I was just learning the art of quilting when I purchased some quilt design software. I was anxious to start using my new computer program and found it to be very straightforward, but my lack of quilting experience was a major hindrance to the design process. Now I'm a huge fan of Dear Jane blocks, the ones based on the dizzying array of geometrics originally sewed by Jane Stickle in Vermont in the mid-nineteenth century. It was a challenge but eventually I designed a quilt packed full of her patterns with the feel of an Irish chain.

With a printout of my impending masterpiece tucked under one arm, I drove to my local quilt shop to pick out fabrics with the enthusiasm of a new mother. But as I wandered among the stacks and shelves of beautiful fabrics, I became more and more confused. Lacking a natural eye for color and a background in quilting, my enthusiasm turned to bewilderment. Then, just when I was feeling hopelessly lost, a very kind and very experienced saleslady approached, asking if I needed help. Her name was Leslie and she was an angel. I showed her my design and asked for help picking out fabric. Leslie was less than enthralled with my design but nonetheless, she set out on a mission to find the perfect fabrics.

I really didn't have any particular color combinations in mind so I just asked Leslie to pick out something that would make my quilt stand out in a crowd. She pulled out a turquoise/purple-mixed fabric, a solid purple, and a yellow-mixed fabric. They were definitely not what I would have picked out for myself but I decided that if Leslie liked them, they must be okay. I purchased my fabric, thanked her, and headed home to create.

About three months after this initial shopping trip, my husband and I packed up our motor home to head south to Florida for the winter. Of course, I took my sewing machine and quilt to work on while we enjoyed the winter sunshine. Under normal living conditions, our motor home is quite comfortable for the two of us, but when I transformed the dining area into a sewing room it became somewhat crowded. However, being a very patient and understanding man, my husband worked around the many scraps of fabric and paper that cluttered the table and floor.

After several hours of paper piecing one morning, I noticed hubby was becoming less tolerant of my creative venture. I figured it was time to put the masterpiece away for a while and turn my attention to him. So I cleaned up the scraps, stowed my machine, and packed away my unfinished treasure. Since it was close to lunchtime, I fixed him one of his favorites—a big, juicy cheeseburger. To my horror, he bit into the sandwich, chewed a couple of times, then stopped to glare at me as he pulled a thread from his mouth. He started to raise his voice but then stopped short, looked at me, and then we both became fairly hysterical with laughter.

As the months in the motor home passed, I finished my quilt top and was extremely pleased with the result. Leslie had picked winning fabrics that I had grown to love as I worked on each block. I was ready to select backing fabric, so I folded up my quilt top and hubby and I headed proudly into town to the local quilt shop. All of the salesladies raved over the pattern and the unusual color combination as I explained that I had purchased the fabrics in Indiana and hoped they had something for the back to complement the unconventional color scheme.

We moved my quilt to a table in a backroom where we spread it out in order to audition potential fabrics. Bolt after bolt piled up beside my quilt and eventually, everyone in the shop became involved in choosing the backing. We were having fun but, once again, I was becoming confused and bewildered. Suddenly I blurted out, "I just wish Leslie were here. She would know exactly what I should use to finish my quilt."

To my astonishment, a voice in the next room said, "Cathy? Is that you?"

I turned to find Leslie standing in the door to the backroom of this quilt shop in Florida, a thousand miles from home. We started screaming and hugging and soon everyone in the shop was gasping, clapping, and hugging. After I regained my composure, I found out that Leslie was vacationing in Florida, had seen this quilt shop and just couldn't pass up the chance to stop in. She had no idea I was there and I had no idea she was visiting from Indiana.

After we all settled down, Leslie did pick out the perfect backing fabric and everyone agreed with her choice. In fact, considering what had just happened, I don't think anyone would have disagreed. Then Leslie left for the airport to fly back to Indiana and I returned to our motor home to sandwich my quilt and commence the hand quilting process.

To this day, I still get chills up my spine whenever I look at this quilt or tell this story. I wonder about fate and exactly what it was that brought Leslie and me together in that quilt shop in Florida so far from home at that moment in time. Oh, if only quilts could talk.

CATHY CARDWELL *is a former industry executive with a lifelong love of fabric and a passion for sewing. She began sewing clothing at a very young age, expanded her sewing to include home decor and accessories af-ter she was married, and branched out into quilting when she retired from her management job. Combining her sewing and computer expertise, she teaches both computerized quilt design and computerized clothing design and construction. Cathy spends numerous hours blending sewing tech-niques for both clothing and quilt construction to design one-of-a-kind clothing, quilts, and home accessories.*

USE IT UP

- - - - -

MARLENE BUSH

Growing up during the Depression meant learning some hard lessons. You lived the "use it up" principle in ways that folks nowadays don't understand and often think bizarre. For example, you saved the wrapper from a stick of margarine to "butter" a cookie sheet, froze overripe bananas to push off on an unsuspecting child as a Popsicle, and saved every worn garment, no matter the fabric, to make quilts.

My mother, Wilma Jewel Light Addison, grew up in that era and in a place that epitomized it. Life in the Ozark Mountains was hard, but as she dealt with the frugalities of life, she developed courage and determination worthy of the bravest soldier. In her family, shoes were saved for winter, books for hungry minds were few and far between, and real cloth rags were used for "that time of the month." But worst of all were the times her father came home drunk. In order to save her from the beatings they all endured, her five older brothers hid Wilma in the woods, where she'd spend the night alone.

She'd only finished the tenth grade in the small school in Lurton, Arkansas, before marrying my father, Arthur Edward Addison. He was working in the nearby Civilian Conservation Corps camp, where he cleared land and helped to build roads for $2 a month for his own pocket and $21 to send to his parents. He'd only finished the sixth grade when his family sent him off to work. Mom was sixteen when they married. Dad was twenty-one.

They had a baby right away and tried to farm in those beautiful but rock-filled mountains. Then World War II began and Dad had to go. So Mama moved to California to live with her mother and work in the fruit packinghouses to save up to buy a farm when Dad got home.

Mama made a lot of quilts in California, both for everyday use and just to pass the time. One of her brothers smoked and she saved the small, muslin drawstring sacks that his tobacco came in. When they'd saved up enough, Mama and Grandma "unsewed" the seams, dyed the fabric, and made two quilts from them. I still have one of them, a gentle reminder of that "use it up" way of life.

The years passed, three more children came, and the lessons learned in childhood were really put to the test. Because she fed four children and her in-laws much of the time, Mama saved every way she possibly could. Quilts were a necessity, and though the patterns were varied, the reality of saving every scrap of fabric meant beauty had to be put aside. They were often large strips of old wool (and eventually double-knit polyester) from garments bought at thrift stores sandwiched using old blankets as batting and tied with leftover bits of yarn. But even with hard use and repeated washings, those double-knit quilts survive today.

Finally, the children were grown and times became a little easier. As a young woman, I remember wondering how in the world my mother could sew for hours while I kept thinking how great it would be to have a little time to just sit and do nothing. I guess all new mothers think the same thing at one time or another.

But Mama simply couldn't sit and be idle. Until the summer she turned seventy-eight, she canned everything Daddy brought in from the garden, worked part-time handing out samples at the grocery store, and saved every scrap of fabric to make quilts.

Her patterns became more elaborate but she continued her well-established habit of cutting a template for every shape and cutting each piece individually. By then, I was quilting too and tried diligently to make life easier for her with tools such as a rotary cutter and a matt. But when I showed her how to use them, Mama just smiled and shook her head. Most of her quilts were hand pieced, all of them were hand quilted, and she continued to use every scrap even when the colors clashed so badly they made your eyes hurt.

That year, I began to notice that the quality of her quilting was deteriorating, at first gradually and then more rapidly. She was just a couple of months short of her seventy-ninth birthday when she began to have seizures. Typical of her stoicism, she told no one, just gritted her teeth and chalked it up to the rigors of her age. Then I began to notice memory losses and even some confusion. Then one day, she told me she stopped to pump gas in her car and discovered she'd left her credit card at Wal-Mart. My mother never used a credit card.

That night, she had another seizure, one that was bad enough for Daddy to notice it and call my sister. A CT scan showed a brain tumor.

Her surgery was long and the prognosis was worse. Two months. If you've never heard anyone say those words then you don't realize that time really does stand still, your heart really does skip a beat, and it's hard to make sense of anything. My family and I took her home with us and settled in to take care of her until the end.

Physically, she recovered rather quickly but mentally, her deterioration, though sometimes subtle, was rapid. But the lessons she learned early in life never left her. She couldn't and wouldn't sit idle. She had to have help walking but she still moved from room to room. In the sunroom, she'd sit and watch the birds she loved so much. In the kitchen, she would look at the paper even when she could no longer read. On the patio, she would stand holding on to a post to watch the clouds, listen to the outdoor sounds, smell the flowers. And in the living room, she would sit on the couch, watch television, and pick up her piecing, sewing quietly as she watched.

She could no longer cut pieces so I cut them for her. She couldn't do anything elaborate but she could sew squares together so I cut hundreds of them. She would stitch Nine Patches, looking each time at the sample one I made for her. Sadly, at the end, even that became frustrating. She would get so confused that she'd sit for minutes at a time staring at the needle, wondering what to do with it.

Those doctors didn't know my mother, didn't know the courage and persistence she'd learned as a child and woman. She lived for a full year after their diagnosis and she pieced quilts until the day she went to bed and didn't get back up, two weeks before she died. She'd been married for over sixty-one years to that young man from the CCC camp who grieved so hard during her illness that he died four months before she did. Hours before she passed away, when she had been in a coma for two weeks, she talked to him one more time saying, "I've had my stuff ready for days. Where have you been?"

I've no doubt her "stuff" included the quilt pieces she carried with her wherever she traveled.

Now you want to know what happened to the Nine Patches Mama sewed that last year, don't you? They're there in my sewing room and in my sister's sewing room until we can still our weeping hearts long enough to put them together into the quilts they will become. Some of them will have the seams reinforced, but only the very last ones she sewed. Others are ready, waiting to become a touchable reminder that life's lessons might be hard but beauty lurks there if you savor the small pieces and stitch them together to make that life a work of art.

MARLENE BUSH *and her husband, Jerry, are both retired educators, and live on beautiful Lake Catherine in Hot Springs, Arkansas. They are the parents of three grown children (all teachers) and the grandparents of seven. She is an adjunct faculty member of Henderson State University, serving as a clinical supervisor of intern teachers, and a trained Stephens Minister volunteering at St. Joseph's Mercy Medical Center. She quilts as often as possible with friends in two groups—the Saline County Quilter's Guild and a small group called Nimble Thimbles.*

A PATCHWORK OF WORDS

The Making of Quilts and Novels

- - - - -

EARLENE FOWLER

People always ask me why I chose quilts and their patterns as the theme for my Benni Harper mystery series. As a marketing tool, choosing quilting would have been brilliant because there are millions of quilters in the world. But, to be honest, I cannot take credit for that brilliance, because I had no idea when I started my series that quilting had become so popular again. I simply wrote about quilts because I love them.

I did not grow up with quilts. In my house, in the Los Angeles suburb town of La Puente, my mother never owned anything except store-bought blankets. She grew up a cotton sharecropper's child during the Depression thirties in southwestern Arkansas. Like many women of her era and background, she associated anything handmade with the rural poverty she was trying to escape. She always found it a bit bewildering when I'd tell her how highly quilters prized the vintage feed-sack material my grandmother used to make dresses for her daughters. So I never learned about quilts from my own mother.

But when we visited her mother, my Grandma Webb, I would be tucked away with my sisters under Grandma's beautiful, colorful quilts. I'd fall asleep under the quilts, listening to stories about our family and the people in the small town where Grandma Webb lived. I think it was then that my connection between quilts and stories began.

I was in my late twenties when I attempted my first quilt. I'd started taking some evening classes at a local community college. One was a writing class, one a fine arts drawing class.

I discovered both a love for writing and an interest in art, though it quickly grew into a love for folk art rather than the fine arts, art that was created by the people I'd come from, the Okies and Arkies who migrated to California after World War II. I started reading about folk art and specifically quilts. I found I was much more interested in the quilters and their lives than in actually learning the various quilting techniques. So after making a few clumsy baby quilts for my niece and nephew, I stopped quilting but continued to read about quilts, their history, and the lives of the quilters themselves.

My Grandma Webb found my interest in why people quilted a bit strange. I think she found the way I displayed the quilts she gave me even stranger because she never thought of her quilts as art. Once, when I was showing her some pictures of my house, she said, "Yep, that's Earlene Susan's house. She still has them blankets hanging on the wall." For the life of her, Grandma Webb couldn't imagine why I would hang blankets on the wall. To her, quilts were always, first and foremost, things to keep you warm.

Until I began my first novel when I was thirty-seven, it never occurred to me to incorporate quilts in my fiction. Like many aspects of my life, I just took them for granted. When I started *Fool's Puzzle,* a mystery set in a folk art museum and concerning a quilt exhibit, it was unnamed.

Halfway through the novel, when I was walking through a local quilt show marveling at the evocative names of the patterns, it occurred to me to name the book after one of them. *Fool's Puzzle* was the perfect metaphor for my story even though I still wasn't thinking in terms of a series. But when I sent the book to an agent in New York to consider, I came up with the idea of naming all the books after quilt patterns. It seemed natural because the pattern names suggested stories to me. Since there are over six thousand quilt patterns with more being added every day, I'll never lack for titles.

It was also at a quilt show that it came to me that quilts are for women like cars are for men. Just as most men appreciate a finely restored automobile, most women, whether or not they've ever threaded a needle in their life, cannot walk by a handmade quilt without stopping to admire its beauty and mystery. Something in quilts speaks to women and connects us—erasing everything that is different and highlighting everything that is the same.

The funniest thing a quilter ever said to me at a book signing was, "How in the world do you ever find the time and patience to write a whole book?"

I asked her, "How long did it take you to piece and quilt your last quilt?"

"About a year," she replied. "And that's working on it a little every day in between my job and laundry and the kids and cooking."

I just smiled and she smiled back. That said it all.

EARLENE FOWLER *was raised in La Puente, California, by a southern mother and a western father. She is the author of the Benni Harper quilt mysteries. She lives in Southern California with her husband, Allen, and her semi-obedient Pembroke Welsh corgi, Boudin ("Boo"). Her Web site is www.earlenefowler.com.*

WHAT IS YOUR SIGN?

– – – – –

ELEANOR FOLLWEILER

I belong to a small group of quilting enthusiasts who originally took a class together and had such a wonderful time, we decided to keep on getting together. We meet once a month, on the first Monday, taking turns hosting the group in our homes. We call ourselves the Monday Morning Fun Bunch and we've been doing this since 1994.

We usually try to bring a lap-sized project to work on and we share photos and other things about our lives. We also bring along food, potluck dishes that serve as our lunch together. This is the best part about getting together and for the most part, our system works out just fine—except for the time we all brought desserts. Thank goodness the hostess of the day had made a pot of soup.

We often choose specific block patterns to make as a group. When the blocks are finished, they are sewn together to make quilt tops, which are then donated to different nonprofit organizations who raffle them off for fund-raisers. So far, our quilt tops have raised money for local libraries, an ambulance corps, and an animal shelter.

Of course, life flows through our group meetings. One year, one of our members died from injuries sustained in a car accident when she was on her way to a quilt-related function. Another member recently lost her husband to cancer; one has a son who was deployed to Iraq and his mother had a lot of "inside" military stories to tell.

As I said, each of us takes a turn hosting the group in her home. Our most senior member, Marian, lives on a farm in a very rural area of our part of Pennsylvania, and the first time her turn came up, her husband, Arlin, made directional signs to help us all find their home. He went to a great deal of trouble to make them nice and each sign sported a different quilt pattern—Ohio Star, Log Cabin, Pinwheel, etc. They were really great-looking signs and got us all to where we were going.

We were just about to share our potluck lunch when there was a knock at the farmhouse door. There were three ladies standing on the stoop, asking, "Is this the quilt shop?"

Laughter immediately broke out when we realized they had been following Arlin's signs. The ladies enjoyed the joke once we explained it to them but declined our invitation to join us for lunch and went on their merry way. About twenty minutes passed and there was another knock at the door. This time it was a mother and a daughter. They also wanted to know: "Is this the quilt shop?"

As before, we all had a good laugh about it but Marian advised Arlin that he'd better go out and fetch his signs. I've often wondered what kind of story those women tell about their search for this "little quilt shop in the country."

ELEANOR FOLLWEILER *is a charter member of the Heart and Home Quilter's Guild of Kutztown, Pennsylvania, served as the guild's first president, and has chaired various guild committees. Her ninety-four-year-old mother is a superb hand quilter and passed the craft along to Eleanor and her six sisters. Her quilting interests have helped her get through her son's deployment to Iraq, something she says is a great challenge. Eleanor and her husband live in the country on a two-acre tract of land, where they take pride in their lawn and their twelve gardens.*

QUILTING FOR LOVE

- - - - -

MAURA C. FLANNERY

I started to quilt because of science, but now I quilt out of love. I teach biology and came up with the idea that there were similarities between science and quilting: both involve putting elements together to create new patterns, both are communal activities, and both require skilled work. I liked this comparison because it has positive feminist connotations unlike most descriptions of science—as conquest, as interrogation of nature—which are more masculine and harsh in tone. Relating science to quilting made science seem more welcoming to women. I wanted to write about this but thought I should actually do some quilting before I committed anything to paper.

From the day I stood at my worktable and began to plan what pattern I would use and what fabrics would be placed where in the pattern, I fell in love with quilting. I realized right away that there was a lot more thought involved than I had ever expected. When I actually started sewing and saw a pattern develop before my eyes, I was hooked. But the part of making a quilt that I came to love most is the actual quilting itself, which I do by hand. To me, each stitch is an expression of the love I am adding to the quilt.

My husband, Bob, was bemused by all this. He was happy to see me so taken up with something aside from work and home. After a hard day, he would sit at the computer playing a card game like hearts or solitaire and I would be close by, sewing. He enjoyed the sound of the thread going through the fabric as

I quilted in a hoop. He found it warm and comforting. To me, it was the sound of the love that I was putting into each stitch.

I gave my first quilt, a wall hanging, to Bob, not only as an expression of love but as a diplomatic maneuver. I figured that he would look more kindly on the money I was spending on my newfound passion if he got something out of it. I then went on to make wall hangings for family and friends. I didn't get up the courage to make a full-sized quilt until after September 11, when I felt the need to make something comforting that we could sleep under. I vividly remember the day I bought the fabric at the City Quilter, my sewing home-away-from-home, in Manhattan. Business wasn't booming so I got a lot of attention, which I needed because I wasn't great at selecting fabrics. I ended up with fabrics that I would never have picked but which turned out to be perfect together. With my shopping bag of fabric, I then walked farther downtown on a lovely evening and met Bob for dinner. It was one of those rare, perfect days.

I finished the quilt the following February, around the time we had our own personal September 11. We found out Bob had colon cancer. I was glad I had a material way to express my love, and that we had something comforting to snuggle up under. Before the surgery, I went into the City Quilter to buy fabric for a very special quilt. I wanted to use the Hawaiian Fleur-de-Lys pattern that I had found in a copy of *McCall's Vintage Quilts*. It is a two-color quilt in the Hawaiian style but instead of one big design, there are twenty blocks with a pattern that includes a fleur-de-lys. Bob taught French history and one of our best trips was to Hawaii, so I thought this was a perfect combination of symbols. I figured that the appliqué would be a good project to take along on all the doctor's visits and waiting that loomed ahead. I was right. I don't think I could have gotten through the hours of the surgery if it weren't for sewing. I just sat there and made stitch after stitch, stitch after stitch, until I was called to the phone and told by the surgeon that things were not good—the cancer had spread out of the colon.

In the following months, through chemo, radiation, and endless tests, I sewed. When I started on the quilt, Bob said he wouldn't live to see it and I worked to prove him wrong—worked at sewing and at doing everything I could to care for him and support him. I finished the quilt by Christmas, and it was a wonderful present to give Bob and to lay on our bed. In the following months, one of the few comforts I had was spreading the quilt over him as both physical and emotional warmth. Bob died on August 3, my parents' wedding anniversary. I left the quilt on the bed but I knew that I couldn't keep it. It was too much of a reminder of too many things. So at Christmas I again wrapped it up as a present. Bob would have had something to say about that: trying to get double mileage out of the same gift! This time I gave it to my sister, Aideen, and her husband, Pat. Aideen had done so much for me through an impossible time that I felt this was the best gift I could give her. They say that a real gift should be difficult to give because it means so much to you, and this quilt fit the bill. It was a way to share with Aideen and Pat the love that Bob and I felt for each other, to, in a sense, not let our love die but pass it on.

I've read about a woman who couldn't continue to quilt after her husband died because quilting was something they had shared, so that it was too painful to do without him. With me, continuing to quilt has been a way to stay sane and find comfort. Before he died, Bob had warned one of our sons not to expect much of an inheritance, because I would be spending it all on quilting! A slight, just slight, exaggeration.

A few months after Bob died, I started to look ahead and worry about how I could face the first anniversary of his death.

Then it dawned on me that the beginning of August might be the time for Quilting by the Lake, the "quilt camp" I had heard so much about at the City Quilter. I had never gone while Bob was alive, because even when he was well, he hated it when I traveled without him. I could get away with short business trips, when he would tell everyone that I had "abandoned" him, but there was no way I would get to go off and quilt for a week.

When I looked up the QBL schedule, it turned out that the second week included August 3. What luck! Bob would definitely be tickled by this. I signed up for Jane Sassaman's class, and of course I had to buy a new sewing machine, keeping in mind that I knew Bob would want me to have the best. So I went off to Quilting by the Lake to create a Floral Fantasy, though I had no idea of exactly what I wanted to do. The night before class began I was reading a novel that mentioned pomegranates as symbols of hope. I couldn't get pomegranates off my mind. This was just what I needed—hope. Four months after Bob died I became quite ill and had rather serious surgery. I was still not fully recovered by August, so a little hope was definitely something I could use. The problem was that I didn't have any photos of pomegranates for inspiration. At one point during the first day of class, I said: "No one has a picture of a pomegranate, do they?" And the woman behind me, Barbara Caldwell, said, "Yes." In fact, she had several photos of pomegranates in her notebook because she had just finished a pomegranate quilt. What luck—or divine intervention! I created a bright, cheerful quilt bursting with pomegranates. Jane Sassaman's patience and artist's eye made it striking.

It is now two years since Bob died, and I am back from another visit to Quilting by the Lake. Last year I bought a pattern for a bed quilt that I knew instantly would be Bob's memorial quilt. I like fabric abstract designs but he liked pictorial prints (we loved each other a lot but also disagreed a lot). This pattern is a country version of a Baltimore Album quilt in which the center square has a house with two swans in front of it. Swans mate for life. This was definitely the quilt to make for Bob. I went out and bought great fabric for it, including a fleur-de-lys print, but I just can't get started on it. The void is still too large. I always find some excuse, some other project, and delay the swans. Right now I'm working on a wedding quilt for the daughter of friends of ours. I am sewing the love of our marriage into something I hope will bless theirs. Bob will just have to wait for his quilt until I sew enough to mend the hole he left, just enough to finally work on the swans.

MAURA C. FLANNERY *is a professor of biology and the director of the Center for Teaching and Learning at St. John's University in Jamaica, Queens, New York.*

IN TRANSLATION

- - - - -

WANDA GUIN

After I'd been quilting for a short time, I started looking for some quilting groups on the Internet to help me improve my techniques and develop some quilting friendships. One of the groups I joined was the Crazyquilters on Yahoo and I'm still amazed at the impact my joining this group had on my family.

I've always enjoyed the fact that the Internet lets you make friends all over the world. There was one lady in the Crazyquilt group who signed her posts "Andrea in Germany" and that really piqued my interest. My father, Enloe Oswalt, was stationed in Germany during World War II, where he met and fell in love with a German girl. Her name was Elizabeth Horn and they wanted to get married, but the military wouldn't let them. They had a baby named Ursula and she was two years old when Dad's enlistment was up. He was ordered back to the States but he couldn't get Elizabeth to come with him, because she didn't want to leave her parents. He left knowing he'd never see Elizabeth or his daughter again.

Over time, he lost contact with them and had not seen his daughter in over fifty years when I started looking for her. I really wanted to find Ursula while Dad was still alive. When I joined Crazyquilters and saw Andrea's byline, I just had to write her and tell her my story. I was so excited when she offered to help find my sister Ursula: I finally had contact with someone who lived there and knew how to do things in Germany.

Andrea explained how to use the online German phone book to find the addresses of people with the name Horn who lived in the Wurzburg area, where my father had been stationed. I sent out twenty letters to those addresses. One of the letters found its way to my half-sister's aunt, Aunt Margarete, and she gave the letter to Ursula. She had thought she would never meet her father nor ever know if she had other family members in America. It was an emotional day when we got an e-mail from Ursula and we immediately knew she was Dad's daughter because he had a picture of her in a baby carriage that he'd carried in his wallet for over fifty years. Ursula described one just like it that had been carried by her mother.

We had finally found her! We e-mailed each other, then called on the phone and talked. A short time later, "Uschi" (a nickname for Ursula) and her husband, Richard, came to America to meet all of us and see the father she didn't remember. That was surely a day none of us will ever forget. There were smiles and tears all around. Uschi showed us the picture of her in her baby carriage that her mother had carried, the duplicate of Dad's.

Dad had turned seventy-seven just before Ursula came to see us and they had a wonderful reunion, talking about their lives and what happened to her mother (she died in the 1990s) and grandparents (who died not long after the war) and aunts. Family members from all over the United States got to meet them and all of us just love Uschi and Richard. It's been wonderful for us to get to know them and their family. Now we have more nieces and nephews to love!

She and Dad talk on the phone every other Sunday, and we e-mail and call each other all the time. My husband became Uschi's granddaughter's second godfather. As you can imagine, the people in my online quilting group, the Crazyquilters, were so excited to read about the whole adventure as it went along. Andrea became our translator, and still translates some for us, although Uschi has learned to write in English fairly well. We could not have found a nicer person to help us find my sister!

We might have never found my sister Ursula if it had not been for a string of circumstances that started with a love of quilting and the compassion of one dedicated quilter, Andrea Stracke.

(In addition to helping people reunite long-lost sisters, Andrea makes beautiful whole-cloth quilts and teaches hand quilting in many parts of Germany. In 2005, some of her work came to the United States with the World Quilting Competition, in which she won first place for her country.)

WANDA GUIN *lives in Memphis, Tennessee, and has been a member of the Uncommon Threads Quilt Guild for several years. Most of her works have been small wall hangings and baby quilts but she is currently working on several large quilts. Sunbonnet Sues and appliqué are among her favorite patterns and techniques.*

HELEN THE HELPER

— — – – — —

MARIAN GOWAN

"I'll find another home for Helen before I move in with you," my mother had said.

"No, don't do that. Helen's your cat. She's been with you for almost ten years. She belongs with you," I responded, thinking of how the shy calico kitten my mother had adopted from the animal shelter had become her constant companion.

"But you have a cat already," she pointed out.

"Yes, and two dogs. They'll learn to get along."

And so it was settled and they both moved into my home. Then, about a month later, my mother died in her sleep. Helen was curled up next to her.

Now when I sew, Helen jumps up next to my machine, purring as she settles into the vibrant colors of jungle animals and star points swimming in a bright green background. With her help, my seams are straighter and my points are pointier.

As I place completed squares on my work table, she re-arranges them, leaving behind strands of fine black and yellow fur as her seal of approval.

Then as I stretch the mottled dark blue backing for the quilt on my dining room table, Helen rolls on one end, kneading the material with her clawless front paws. As I spread the layer of batting, she nestles into the cloud of soft cotton.

When the top is in place, Helen watches me pin baste each section to make the quilt sandwich—top, batting, and bottom—ready for machine quilting. There's another soft, curling motion about the star points, another deposit of fine fur, another sign of her approval.

Now all the machine quilting is done, and as I sit whipstitching the binding into place, Helen snuggles into a completed side. She moves begrudgingly as I pull the quilt out from under her to finish the next edge.

I know Helen won't be happy when I mail this quilt to my daughter. But my stash beckons. Soon she will be helping with another.

MARIAN GOWAN, *a graduate of Northfield Mount Hermon School and Jackson College of Tufts University, discovered quilting and writing after retiring from her thirty-year career in corporate America. She is a member of the Western Carolina Quilters Guild and volunteers with the Blue Ridge Literacy Council in North Carolina, tutoring English as a second language.*

SUNNY

– – – – –

FONDA L. SARFF

I met Sunny in a hardware store in my hometown in the early 1970s. She was new in town, with a bright, fiery personality, and although I was terminally shy at the time, we hit it off right away. Both our families had a sewing history.

Could we have ever guessed what we'd go through together?

Back then, I sewed all my own clothes and a lot for my family. That was cool with Sunny. When I succumbed to too many PBS quilting shows and started quilting, she stood by me. Together, we went through two houses, four dogs, seven cats, three sewing machines, and innumerable renovations of sewing rooms.

We learned strip piecing and how to appliqué using freezer paper. We made miles and miles of bias for Celtic appliqué and quilt bindings. We made gifts, raffle quilts, and miniatures. She was even there by my side when I made my first Lone Star quilt with all those diamonds. (What a challenge that was!)

Through all my successes and disasters, Sunny was there. When I quilted through long, snowy afternoons, she was there. When I couldn't sleep because I was so worried about my mother's Alzheimer's and sewed till 3 A.M., Sunny helped me through. She even stayed up with me when I pulled that all-nighter to make an entry deadline for a quilt show.

Then the other day, I made my usual call for help but there was no reply. After all those years with her at my elbow, Sunny did not answer the call and I was on my own. Sunny was gone. I'd had no idea things were so serious. Oh, she'd been getting slower as she aged, but aren't we all? I suppose I thought we would sew together forever.

Will I go on? Yes. Will I make new sewing friends? Yes. But they won't be Sunny. There'll never be another like her, my Sunbeam Shot of Steam Model 11-104 iron.

FONDA L. SARFF *is a native of north Idaho who helped establish the Panhandle Piecemakers Quilt Guild. The challenge and satisfaction of creation from design to last stitch fuels her love of quilting, and she refuses to limit herself to one method or style of quiltmaking. She has too many hobbies—all of which take a backseat to quilting—several cats, a Welsh dog, and a father she adores who not only puts up with her fabric addiction but is always willing to "take a look" and share an opinion.*

SNOWFLAKES

- - - - -

NIÑA KLINCK

 At the same time I discovered quilting, I was also a budding paper cutter, mostly of snowflakes. Growing up in Vermont, you would always see paper snowflakes plastered on someone's winter window and our house was no exception. As I got older, I discovered that origami paper is the perfect cutting medium. It's thin and tough and you can make cuts that not only repeat well, you can also cut away most of the paper and leave a remarkably fine snowflake.

As my quilting skills grew along with my paper-cutting skills, I found myself trying to figure out how to make these same delicate snowflakes in fabric. To me, the most perfect snowflakes are the huge, fluffy ones that drift so slowly out of the sky, you can almost see their six sides while they descend and that's what I wanted to replicate in my quilting. I tried lots of different techniques—piecing, paper piecing, Hawaiian appliqué, reverse appliqué, fusible appliqué—but none of them made a snowflake with the delicate beauty I was seeking.

Finally, my memory recalled some Hungarian felt cutwork I'd seen at a craft show and the wheels started turning. Wool felt! It brought back memories of the only quilts I had known as a youngster. They were made from the scraps of men's wool suit coats and were left behind by a man who boarded with us. My mother replaced their backings with red flannel and retied them but they didn't make it past my teenage years. I've since discovered that they were made in Beeville, Texas, by that man's grandmother during the 1920s.

Now that I knew what I wanted to try, I alerted my mother, also known as the "Bag Lady," to be on the lookout for suit coats with no less than 85 percent wool content when she made her weekly trips to Listen, one of our local secondhand stores. It took two years of gathering (often by the trash bag load) and felting (in my washer and dryer—oh, what a mess!), cutting (long nights watching movies while I removed usable buttons and usable parts from the coats and pants), ironing, and cutting again before I had enough wool felt to make a full-sized quilt.

In the fall of 2003, on a quilter's retreat, I took my bag of precut scraps and (mostly) white wool felt, and proceeded to piece and cut and piece and cut. The final product was a wool quilt with beautiful snowflakes of all different sizes floating over its top. I finished it just in time for Christmas and gave it to my brother and his wife for their new home. My gift came with one stipulation, however. It had to be available to show at a few national events over the next year.

My snowflake quilt eventually traveled to six shows and won five ribbons, including Judge's Choice and Best Use of Recycled Materials. At the same time, I decided to take my very first quilting class with Harriet Hargrave, a renowned quilting author and teacher. Her unabashed love of quilting inspired me and I went from quilting by hand to tying quilts to having my aunt quilt my projects on her long arm machine to finally learning how to quilt my own endeavors on my home machine with confidence.

Since then, I've taught my own classes, showing others my snowflake technique, and I'm in the process of writing a book about it. There are two other snowflake quilts still drifting about in my mind, waiting their turn to be realized. In my search for the perfect snowflake, I discovered how to piece my own landscapes and appliqué my own stories using embroidery, silk ribbon, reverse appliqué, and trapunto. I've fallen in love with whole cloth quilts and design my own, combining my paper-cutting and machine-quilting skills. I am now exploring free-motion machine quilting with all the beautiful new threads that are available today.

Though I've been involved with quilting for more than twenty-five years, I still feel as though I am only at the beginning of this journey and have far to go. I look forward to all the discoveries waiting for me. Not only am I gaining skill and knowledge, I have met the most incredible women along the way.

And that is the true beauty of quilting.

NIÑA KLINCK *lives in tiny Tunbridge, Vermont, with her two children and eight sewing machines, where she sews and teaches handwork such as quilting, paper cutting, temari, and wheat weaving, among other crafts. She discovered sewing as a seven-year-old but didn't really find her passion for quilting until the 1970s. She works in a nursery, where she finds much inspiration for her quilts in the plants. She is currently trying to bring sewing—particularly quilting—back to the classrooms of middle schools. You may write to her in Tunbridge—it will get there!*

SHOPPING FOR BATIKS ON SALE

with James Joyce on My Mind

- - - - -

TSANI MILLER

Wise old Ellen waddled from the backroom bearing a bolt of batik in purples and blues with swags of yellow silk and scarlet satin stretched over and under one another dangling from her neck. The pockets of her patchwork jacket, filled with pincushions and tape measures and spools of thread, gaped and bobbled like squirming puppies as she swayed in my direction, the uncertain and certain customer. She slid the fabrics over the counter and under my nose and intoned:

"These are the colors that you like the best. These are the ones that are on sale."

I stopped my fingers in full caress on flocked gingham that reminded me of the curtains my aunt on K Street once told me were guardians against the world when she drew them tight, and I peered at Ellen across the brightly lit room full of fluorescence.

"For this I drove one hundred miles in one day?"

Old Ellen smiled and the action robbed her cheeks of their soft smoothness until I could see the merchant part of her grin visible and heard the crash of the cash register in her heart because she knew that no quilter can long resist the allure of hand-dyed batiks on sale for only $3.99 per yard. She gave a low whistle and the front door of the store opened and a multi-mob of fellow quilters came pouring in over the threshold, came running and ambling and dangling cloth bags and wearing T-shirts that said: Whoever dies with the most fabric wins. And I knew I was lost and threw myself on top of the bolt and intoned in my best yearning quilter's voice:

"For this I drove one hundred miles in one day."

Then she smiled down on me and would have stroked my hair if I let her but the others were scrambling over the cloth and I knew that if I wanted to empty my wallet and leave my cash in a place where it would be well taken care of, I had to act now while I still had a chance.

"Tell me, Ellen," I said in despair.

"Yes, my dear?"

"Will my desire for the perfect fabric ever be satisfied?"

She smiled her biggest smile at that and intoned:

"Oh no, my dear. Never."

I sighed because I was glad she was right.

"I'll take it," I said.

When TSANI MILLER *was born, in Los Angeles, her mother gave her the first name Annie but Tsani changed it when she left home at age eighteen to look for adventure. At this point, she's been around the world twice. She currently quilts in Atlanta, but don't expect to find her there if you go looking, because she is always restless. Tsani likes to channel famous writers when she writes and wishes she could meet Jane Austen.*

NICARAGUAN FABRIC CONNECTION

— — — — —

ELLIE MACNEIL

Have you ever left on an adventure with preconceived ideas only to have all of them fly out the window and be replaced by a totally unexpected experience? Well, this happened to me.

We left the bitter cold of a Canadian winter in February 2004, and within hours arrived at our destination, Nicaragua. I was accompanying a group of university students whose purpose for the trip was to talk with selected groups of people in order, hopefully, to get a better understanding of life in a Third World country.

During our stay, we spent time in Managua, the capital. We met with groups working hard to improve the living conditions of the people. We talked with women who worked unbelievably long and arduous hours in the sweatshops that produce the expensive clothes we buy so readily here at home. We spoke with children fortunate enough to be able to afford the school uniform that is their ticket to an education. Many were delighted to practice their English on real gringos. We practiced our Spanish on them.

I had hoped to meet with a group of women who quilted when we flew to the Caribbean coastal town of Puerto Cabezas. I had seen some of their work in Canada and was quite excited to meet and visit with them. But then I was told that the meeting was not going to take place, because the women had no fabric.

No fabric! I could not comprehend having no fabric. I could visualize my stash at home, resting quietly in neat piles awaiting my return. I was quite disappointed. The following days were filled with more meetings and visiting various community projects but I could not get it out of my mind—no fabric.

Upon my return to Canada, I set to work. I talked to the ladies of my own quilt guild and I presented the situation to other quilt guilds. Soon beautiful cotton fabrics began to arrive at my home. Sometimes I would open my door and find a box of wonderful fabrics that had been left there by some unknown quilter friend. Other boxes were left at stores in a nearby town, ready for me to pick up at my convenience. It seemed the whole community was getting on board.

Money was also donated to help cover the cost of shipping. I would meet friends in town or at church and often a $20 bill would be discreetly slipped into my hand "for your ladies in Nicaragua." At the meeting of one quilt guild, my car was filled so full of donated cotton fabric that one lady offered to take the overflow and deliver it to me at church on Sunday. Soon my quilting loft was piled high with donated fabric and sewing supplies. I was running out of room to do my own sewing! What a wonderful dilemma to be in!

In little over a year after my initial visit to Nicaragua, 440 pounds of donated fabric, scissors, needles, thread, and embroidery floss have been shipped to the quilters. I also include a disposable camera in some of the bales of fabric. The ladies in Nicaragua take pictures and return the camera to me since there is no place to develop film in their little village. I get double prints made and return one set to Nicaragua, using my set of photos in my presentations.

In 2004, my Fabric Connection project began sending fabric and sewing supplies to one group of ten ladies in Puerto Cabezas.

This quickly grew to two groups with between fifteen and twenty ladies in each group. Soon, another group was formed in an out-lying village. It wasn't long before a fourth group was set up in yet another outlying village in a very poor area. There is no road to this fourth location, no electricity, and no source of potable water within the village itself.

I don't need to tell fellow quilters how it feels to work on a project and complete it so you can see the final results! But in Nicaragua quilting sessions also serve another important pur-pose: they give the women in these villages a gathering place. Hus-bands frown on their wives gathering to just socialize. However, if they are producing something, better yet producing something to sell, it is another story completely.

Quilting time must be worked around the daily chores of these women, since where they go, their young children also go. These chores, such as laundry, cooking, and obtaining food, whether in the market or from other sources, take much of their day because of the lack of modern amenities that we take for granted. This puts difficult parameters around the time and place of their quilting sessions.

The women sell their goods locally in markets. They've sent some of their pieces to me and I treasure each and every one. When I showed some of the work of these Nicaraguan quilters at a guild meeting, one lady jumped up and shouted, "That's the fabric I sent down!" How wonderful to see this project come full circle and to imagine the joy our excess fabric has brought to our quilting sisters in Nicaragua!

ELLIE MACNEIL *lives in Norland, Ontario. Her Fabric Connection is an ongoing project. For more information about Ellie's project, you can contact her at elliem@sympatico.ca.*

SEEK TO PURCHASE MISSION

- - - - -

JOANN ABBOTT

Years ago, when my family was stationed in Germany, my husband decided to do some early Christmas shopping for me. He knows that fabric is always the perfect gift but the problem was, back then, that Germany had virtually no fabric shops for quilters. In fact, there were only two located anywhere near us—a mini one in our local PX and a much bigger one, a "real" quilt and crafts shop, way over on the East German border, in Grafenwehr, I think.

Scott was not deterred, however, and waited for his chance to shop for me. He got his opportunity that fall when he was sent on a two-week training mission near the big quilt shop. At some point, he was able to get away from his war games for some private recon and purchase activities.

Dressed in what is called "full battle rattle"—helmet, fatigues, web vest and harness, a weapon across one shoulder, and camouflage makeup on his face—he walked into the arts and crafts center, heading for the fabric. A lady behind the counter came around to help him, figuring he must be lost and looking for the automotive area next door.

"Can I help you with something, Sergeant?" she asked, ready to steer him to the guy stuff next door.

He said the stunned look on her face was wonderful as he replied, "I am looking for some one-hundred-percent cotton fabric to give to my wife. Do you have any tone-on-tone prints, especially white on white or black on black?"

She recovered, I'm glad to say, and on Christmas morning, I got a pizza box (which was a really sneaky way to pack fabrics— I had no idea what was in it) full of ten yards of various tonal prints, a new cutting matt, a rotary cutter, and a sharpener. Needless to say, he got lots of hugs and kisses in return.

JOANN ABBOTT *has been "sane" quilting for fifteen years and crazy quilting for the last eight. She has been a member of the local quilt guild in every place her family has been stationed—the Cabin Branch Quilters in northern Virginia, the Rheinland/Pfalz Quilters in Kaiserslautern, Germany, and the Hummingbird Stitchers in Sierra Vista, Arizona. She loves bright colors, shiny objects, her husband, and her kids.*

TAKING THE LONG WAY HOME

- - - - -

CATHERINA HOLLIFIELD

With a sigh, I looked up from the quilting book I'd bought during our weekend trip to Chicago. "I'm so glad we're going home. I want to practice some of these new quilting techniques," I said to my husband.

"Oh," he deadpanned.

My heart plummeted. From experience, I knew that the tone of Robert's voice meant my arrival home would be delayed—a lot. On our trips back home to central Illinois, he often experiments with driving different routes to see places he's never seen before. I usually accept these eccentric deviations in our journeys without a fuss. But this time, I just wanted to get home to play in my sewing room. Little did I know the impact his spontaneous decision and our subsequent argument would have on a young mother's life.

"I'm going home a new way, dear," Robert was saying. "It should only add an hour to our travels."

"If you're bored, I'll take over driving," I offered, hoping to deter his detour. "I just want to get home."

But he flatly refused. "It's not that. I'll drive. I just want to take a different route."

Though normally even-tempered, I lost my patience with him, and said things I regretted the minute they left my lips. In turn, my usually agreeable husband adamantly insisted on driving the new route, risking even more displeasure on my part.

Left with only one option, I pouted.

An exaggerated sense of displeasure draped itself over our car like a heavy woolen blanket, suffocating us in our air-conditioned comfort. Silence reigned glorious in our mutual fury.

Eventually, feeling guilty for being nasty, I bit the bullet and attempted to initiate a conversation. I acknowledged my mistake in demanding to go home, admitting I would not have been able to try the techniques in my book because I didn't have certain supplies recommended in it. Admitting I was wrong wasn't easy for me, but Robert remained stubbornly silent.

I knew from experience that he would relent if I kept talking and the tension gradually eased. But I still resented him stealing an hour of my time without permission.

As we drove through a small town, Robert suddenly slammed on the brakes and veered into a shopping center parking lot. "There's a forty percent sale sign on that fabric store. We're stopping so you can buy things to work with."

Irrationally, I refused to leave the car even though he offered me a perfect opportunity to purchase the supplies I needed. "Why can't we just go home?" I demanded.

My mild-mannered husband barked, "You wanted to shop so you're going to shop if I have to drag you in there by the ear."

Stung by his uncharacteristic and vehement outburst, I spitefully decided to visit the store, just for a moment, and then walk out without a purchase.

He parked the Blazer quite a distance from the store under some trees. "It's hot and I want to be in the shade," he said. "Besides, you're a big girl. You can walk that far."

I glared. "All right. I'll be back soon." Seething with indignation, I stalked toward the building.

A young mother and her child were sitting on the grass in front of the store. Her nervous manner attracted my attention.

She was darting anxious looks behind her as she frantically packed her baby's belongings into a diaper bag. A dirty, unkempt man had circled behind her and was obviously attempting to get closer.

Instantly, my perception of the world narrowed to focus on them. The man's queer behavior filled me with dread. What's he up to? I wondered with apprehension as I hastened toward them.

By this time, the woman had risen from the grass and was striding purposefully toward the store but the man did not stop. He was rapidly closing the distance between them and I knew trouble lay ahead. I was hot and sweaty in the oppressive August heat, but I felt an inner coldness the likes of which I'd never felt before. I quickened my pace.

Suddenly, the man realized I was approaching at a rapid clip. He veered from his pursuit, turning to wander aimlessly into the parking lot, hands in his pockets, whistling nonchalantly. Out of shape and gasping for breath, I trembled like a bunny that had just eluded a circling hawk. My heart almost burst with elation when the creep left without incident.

The mother entered the store ahead of me and stood just inside the door, looking out. I initially walked past her without a word, my mind racing. What would she have done if I hadn't scared that guy off? I stopped abruptly and turned back to ask, "Are you okay, miss?"

Her outwardly calm expression melted into a grimace of shock. "Did you think he meant to hurt me?" she asked.

"Yes, but it's okay, dear," I replied. "I would have helped you. My husband was in the car and he would have been there in a second if we needed him."

I gripped her shoulder tightly for a moment in reassurance then smiled and entered the store. The hair on my forearms stood at attention and cold chills rippled down my back as I realized how close this woman had come to potential danger.

When I got back to the car, Robert and I discussed the situation. He'd seen the man and had just opened the car door when the tramp wandered off. "That woman's guardian angel worked overtime on this one," he said. "Imagine what might have happened if we weren't here."

I smiled. "Do you think the next time a guardian angel needs our help, she could just ask instead of causing such a ruckus between us?"

He smiled, too, and gave me a long, reassuring hug. "Making up isn't so bad, is it?"

CATHERINA HOLLIFIELD *learned to love and make quilts after she got married and left home in 1979. She never realized she'd grown up with quilts. When she did discover quilting she thought it was something new. Since then, she's made 275-plus baby quilts, 15 large quilts, and innumerable wall hangings. She often uses her quilting skills to help raise money for charity.*

THE PERFECT GIFT

- - - - -

SHANNON DAY

Every year, I look forward to the time when the local quilt guilds in my city host their annual quilt show. I especially enjoy viewing all the small quilts donated for the show's silent auction, a fund-raiser for local charities. I always save this part for last, taking the time to savor all the full-sized quilts before wandering through the smaller ones. Some of the diminutive quilts are bite-size versions of their bigger cousins and it's fun to put them together. I also check for friends' signatures on the blocks, identify patterns and fabrics, and generally appreciate the creativity of using lone blocks to make small quilts for the silent auction.

One year, as I was making my annual pilgrimage through the silent auction section of the show, I saw quilts with autumn leaves, batik stars, appliquéd cats, and a wide variety of Christmas patterns. Suddenly, as I rounded a corner, a bright and cheery quilt of pure colors popped out at me. It was an appliqué of a house framed by various black-and-white prints. The detail that caught my eye was the fabric in the house's windows. It had been specially placed so that each window had a smiling sun peeking through.

It was called *The Sunshine House* and although I don't usually bid on these quilts, I decided to ask about this one. Much to my surprise, the last bid was only $10. I thought it would make a perfect birthday gift for a friend of mine so I placed the next bid.

At closing, I went back to check on "my" quilt and was

delighted to find out it was, indeed, mine. As the successful bidder, I happily took my find home and showed it to my husband. But instead of appreciating my new purchase, he looked plainly puzzled.

"Isn't that one of the quilts that you donated to the silent auction?" he asked.

You can imagine how I felt as I sheepishly replied, "Well, it was a bargain at $15 and besides, it was for a good cause."

SHANNON DAY *is a Honeybee Quilt Guild member in Jacksonville, Florida. She enjoys making original quilts for family, friends, and charity groups. Some friends call her the "Quilter Realtor" because she provides the same personal touch in her real estate practice. She also helps coordinate quilt making and distribution for various local charities. If you would like to learn more or participate, please e-mail Shannon at quilterrealtor@ earthlink.net.*

QUILTER'S STASH

- - - -

LAUREL KINDLEY

quilter's stash: *a collection of fabric that you tell yourself you're going to use some day but the truth is, you just like to take it out once in a while and look at it.*

When I started looking around my hometown of Richmond, Missouri, for a location for my dream quilt shop, it seemed as if everything the realtors took me to see was either in a bad location, had no parking, or had a price tag that was much bigger than I could afford. Then I found this building that had been on the market for over a year without a single offer. It was small (about eighteen hundred square feet) but cheap. It also had a nice big parking lot and my children would be going to school only two blocks away. So except for the fact that I thought it was the ugliest little store in the world, it was perfect.

I almost didn't know where to begin renovating. The roof and walls leaked. The porch was very run-down with ugly concrete steps and a wood-shingled roof. There was this dark paneling throughout the entire building. The carpet in the main room was dark green with a big tear in the middle; the office and reception areas had this stained brown and orange carpet. At least I think that was the color.

But it was my dream come true so I rolled up my sleeves and got to work.

The building was already equipped with a burglar alarm but the back door needed to be armed. I called the alarm company and they sent a small crew over to check out the wiring. There's a dropped ceiling in the shop and the wires for the alarm ran above that. The crew set up a ladder, lifted one of the ceiling tiles, and to everyone's surprise, three bags of marijuana fell down at our feet.

We stood there, stumped, for several minutes, trying to figure out what to do next. Then we called the police. Since no one knew how long the marijuana had been hidden in that ceiling, the police weren't too concerned about our find, but they took the three bags away and told us that if we found any more, to just throw it away.

We did find another fifteen bags of marijuana during the building renovations, and my contractor threw them away. Then he had three blasting caps fall out of the ceiling and hit him in the chest. When we called the police about that incident, they said the caps had enough explosive to take off a finger or two, and they took the caps away in a special box. During the course of our conversation, I mentioned we had found several more bags of marijuana in the ceiling, and one of the officers said to let him know if more turned up so he could use them for training his dogs.

You have to admit that this gives a whole new meaning to the term "quilter's stash."

LAUREL KINDLEY *was the owner and sole proprietor of the quilt shop I'd Rather Be Quilting, located in Richmond, Missouri, which closed in 2006. She has been married to Chuck for more than ten years and has two* daughters, Rachel and Brianna. Laurel holds a bachelor's degree in Management Information Systems and, before opening her shop, worked for eleven years as a software developer. She's been a quilter for nearly that long. Since closing her software store, she has returned to that career.

HIDING FABRIC MY WAY

- - - - -

When I first began quilting and didn't know any better, I bought only fat quarters when I wasn't purchasing exact amounts of fabric for specific projects. Now contrary to what some of you may be thinking, a fat quarter has nothing to do with a hog's anatomy. No, no, no! Rather it's a piece of fabric a half-yard long and half the width of the fabric wide. In other words, it's cloth cut to approximately 18×22 inches, a size that lends itself easily to lots of different quilting techniques. For those of you who like to e-mail or write about quilting to other quilters, this common cut of cloth is often abbreviated with the letters *FQ*.

The influence of more experienced quilters changed my buying habits and soon those little plastic Baggies of FQs that I used to bring home from the quilt shop were replaced by industrial-strength garbage bags filled with yards—and even bolts—of fabric. I was told that every new quilter must have frequent S.E.X. No, not sex but S.E.X.—Stash Enhancement eXperiences. I plunged into this new way of buying with abandon.

Fortunately for the size of our credit-card bills, that necessary but rather costly phase of my quilting life is now over for me, for the most part. However, now I have to live with the aftermath of my S.E.X. and my little sewing room can't contain all that fabric.

If you live with a significant other who does not quilt, you're going to have a hard time hiding your stash if you buy anything more than FQs. I mean, you can use FQs for bra padding, but bolts of fabric are a much bigger challenge. Now my hubby may be different from others, but normally if an object isn't in his lap or front and center on the top shelf of the refrigerator, he can't find it. Consequently, I don't worry about hiding fabric. But I do need places to store it. The following are some of the more creative ways I've found to do that.

Anything stationary that can be covered with a "skirt" of fabric is a great potential stashing spot. For example, if your house needs a few extra end tables to put "stuff" on—and whose doesn't—buy the biggest plastic garbage cans you can find. Fill them up with fabric, artistically drape more fabric on top, making sure it reaches the floor, add potted plants and lamps or candles, and voilà! End tables with a secret!

Get creative—buy four garbage cans, a sheet of plywood, and make a new dining room table.

The area between the mattress and box spring of all the beds in your house will hold more fabric than you might imagine. The added advantage of this is, of course, firmer mattresses for a better night's rest.

Sofas and chairs with removable seat cushions make good spots to stash your stash, provided your hubby or others in the home don't regularly go diving for loose change there.

Make really big floor cushions for the kids. Use Velcro or zipper closures for easy access, then line them with all that new batting you just bought and stuff with fabric. The dogs could use new beds too, right?

Don't forget the freezer. Wrap your fabric purchases in butcher paper and mark the packages BEEF BRAINS, or anything else you know your husband wouldn't eat even if he were a *Fear Factor* finalist. It will be safe, bug free, and never touched.

From January until November, fabric may be safely stored in anything marked CHRISTMAS DECORATIONS. Just remember to remove the fabric or label the containers SUMMER CLOTHES before the annual transformation of your house into a winter wonderland.

Anywhere you store your undies or lingerie is prime hiding territory unless hubby happens to be a cross-dresser. In that case, you have bigger problems than fabric concealment.

Linen closets are another good spot—when was the last time he changed the sheets? And any box or bag marked "feminine hygiene products" is perfect for stashing fabric—or anything else, for that matter. No self-respecting man ever opens those containers.

The trunk of your car, especially if it's a big sedan like the ones driven by the bad guys in *The Sopranos*—you know, the kind that will hold several bodies—is perfect unless you happen to have a flat while touring the countryside on a Sunday afternoon with hubby. If that should occur, be prepared to show him how you learned to change a tire all by yourself in the Women's Independent Living class you attended, so he doesn't have to get out of the front seat. (You did attend, didn't you?)

Speaking of driving, that reminds me of traveling and that reminds me to ask—what's in your luggage? If you're not traveling, then it's empty. Don't let your suitcases stay that way.

Okay, there you have a few of my favorite fabric storage/hiding tips. They should provide a good starting point for you and may spark other ideas. Just look around, call on your creative muse, and remember that every void can be filled.

BECKY SUNDERMAN *lives in the peaceful foothills of the Ozark Mountains with her loving and very supportive husband and their three miniature schnauzers. She began quilting in hopes of leaving a part of her to this world after her only son was killed in an automobile accident. She now enjoys dyeing and painting fabrics, which she uses in her quilts. Becky feels that God has truly blessed her.*

THIS GUY MUST BE NUTS

- - - - -

GEORGE SICILIANO

Hi folks,

I'm one of the minority of men I know who quilts and as such, I'm often asked how I got started. My story begins with my love of music. I was a member of the United States Marine Drum & Bugle Corps in Washington, D.C., in the early 1960s. After I completed my enlistment, my wife, Virginia, and I bought and ran a music store in Port Jefferson Station, New York. But I've always loved marching in parades, so in 1990 I joined a senior firehouse drum and bugle corps, which gave me the opportunity to not only get out of our store for a few hours, but to march in many of the firemen's parades prevalent on Long Island in the summertime.

Then in 1997, I was diagnosed with diabetes. As a result of the associated leg problems, marching in parades was impossible and I had to resign from the drum and bugle corps.

Now Virginia is an award-winning hand quilter and I have always been in awe of her talent, and especially how she makes it look so easy. As anyone who's ever owned a retail store knows, you don't get much free time and Virginia loves to make quilts with hers. At the time, we kept a book called *Sewing on the Line* on a shelf in our bathroom right next to that big white "porcelain thing." One day, I was looking at it and found a picture of a quilt made with an uneven Log Cabin block that I thought was pretty cool. So after all was said and done, I suggested to

Virginia that she make that quilt for me . . . perhaps today . . . right now?

Before I go on, I must tell you that my wife would do anything for me, and I'm sure that if she hadn't had several quilts in progress with the added pressure of fast-approaching deadlines, she would have made that quilt top immediately. To me, it did not seem like a big request, because it was only sixteen blocks. Her reply, however, made me feel as though I might have just stepped over that "imaginary line" that should become more evident as a marriage progresses in years. I'm going to paraphrase her words here but before I do, I can tell you that her answer to my request, while emphatic and including a number of very descriptive adjectives, started what turned out to be the beginning of my quilting career. That said, her reply was: "IF YOU LIKE IT SO MUCH, MAKE IT YOURSELF!"

What's a guy to do? I reached down and picked up the box that held the brand-new Bernina sewing machine that we had purchased for her the night before. Just to give you a time frame, this was the weekend, Labor Day 1997, that Princess Diana died. Virginia was not feeling well (which may have been the cause of her highly charged reply to my seemingly innocent request) and was curled up on the sofa in the next room, watching the events unfold in England. I set up her sewing machine then stole a few pieces of fabric from her "stash." (Okay, okay out there, please stop yelling. I know—I mean I found out—what that means and I will never, never, never do it again, never. Just forgive me— Virginia did.)

I then proceeded to "operate" this newfound piece of "equipment." What can I say—it's a "guy thing"—we guys love operating equipment! Unfortunately, I kept breaking needles, lots of needles. Did you know that when you start pushing all of those buttons on a Bernina to make various stitches, you have to change the presser foot to match the stitch? I didn't know that, but I found out.

The quilt I wanted to make was "foundation pieced." This is a wonderful method for sewing consecutive pieces of fabric together. To start, the design is transferred onto a foundation material, usually paper, muslin, or a cloth stabilizer. If paper is used, it's called "paper piecing" and the paper must be removed when the quilt is done. If muslin or a stabilizer product is used, it's called "foundation piecing" as the foundation is not removed and becomes a permanent part of the quilt. These terms are often interchanged.

Once the pieces are ready to put together, you simply make a straight seam or "sew on the line." The results of this method are speed and accuracy. Not all quilt blocks lend themselves to this method, but fortunately for me, the Log Cabin block is perfect for this technique.

One thing led to another and now Viriginia and I both quilt. In fact, we share a studio in Lebanon, Pennsylvania, and, as of this writing, we are still talking to each other. The only real precaution I had to take was in the setup of our studio. From her seat, she cannot possibly reach my throat with the rotary cutter and I cannot reach hers. Kidding aside, we spend many quality hours in this room, sharing ideas and just being together.

As time went on, I started making my blocks smaller and smaller because I was curious to see how small I could go. The smallest blocks I ever put in a quilt are three-quarters of an inch square and there are thirty-three pieces of gradated color twirling within that space. These blocks are the centers in my quilt called *Ribbons and Hues*.

When people started seeing what we were up to, quilting guilds started asking Virginia and me to do presentations and workshops. We developed a rather humorous trunk show presentation—this is supposed to be fun, right?——and a workshop with lots of new techniques and tips. We called the trunk show presentation and workshop "Size Really Does Matter." One day, after a presentation, I overheard one quilter say to another: "This guy must be nuts," and I thought, "WOW, what a great name for our presentation." However, I still call the original miniature quilt workshop "Size Really Does Matter." And, indeed it does!

GEORGE SICILIANO *is relatively new to the world of quilting. He is an award-winning maker of miniature quilts, a lecturer, and a teacher. In a rather short period of time, he has developed some of his own techniques and refined some of the basics. He has taken the Log Cabin pattern to new heights by developing and cataloging over 150 different variations of this wonderful and versatile block. Some of George's more recent works can be seen on his Web site, www.georgesiciliano.com. One of them, called* Violet Tendencies, *has 3,450 pieces in a quilt only 9¾ inches square. Information for George and Virginia Siciliano's workshops and presentations can also be found on their Web site or they can be reached by e-mail at georgesiciliano@comcast.net.*

INTERIOR DECORATION

— — — —

JUDY BOWDEN

After a close relationship of almost twenty years, I married and moved into my new husband's home. Before the wedding, we had agreed that I could redecorate and convert the interior of his home from "men's dorm-style hodgepodge" to my preference of "antique French country with lots of color." I have a background in many diverse fields, including interior design, so you can imagine how anxious I was to get started.

For the first few weeks of married life, we slept beneath an unzipped sleeping bag that had served as his bedspread for many years. That old and torn sleeping bag was just too much for a new bride but I knew it would take months for me to find the time to set up a work space to make my own quilt and I just couldn't wait that long. So I purchased a lovely bargello patchwork in pastels of blue, rose, and white, complete with matching pillow shams.

And then I waited for him to notice what I had done.

I waited for two weeks but he never said a word. So I thought maybe he didn't like it or thought it was too feminine, though he hadn't objected to my teddy bears. Finally, when he didn't pick up on the hints I was dropping, I led him into the bedroom and asked if he noticed anything.

He looked around and after a while, he said, "No, I don't smell anything."

I gulped and pointed to the quilt. That's when he finally realized that his old sleeping bag was missing. He assured me that he liked the bargello patchwork and then asked if I'd made it.

I responded, "Of course, last night while you were at your meeting."

I should explain that my husband is clueless about quilts and honestly has no idea how long it takes to make one. But this is not necessarily a fault, because he also has no idea about the size of my fabric stash (packed away in boxes) or the money I have invested in fabrics, quilting supplies, etc.

And I don't intend to shock him with that information.

JUDY BOWDEN *has been interested in quilts since 1971 when she first moved to rural Vermont. She is a member of the Northern Lights Quilt Guild in Lebanon, New Hampshire, and readily admits to being addicted to fabric.*

A THING OF BEAUTY

- - - -

MOLLY WOLF

 It sits, tightly furled, on the shelf in my bedroom closet, a presence, an embarrassment. Frankly, I have no idea what to do with it.

When her son and I got married, my mother-in-law created this quilt for us. It is the Wedding Ring pattern. It's appliqué, not pieced. Each block has a center of four hearts, tip-to-tip, forming a flowerlike core around which circles a wreath of leaves, linked by a run of embroidered stem stitch. She edged the quilt with neat but toothlike triangular jags of white cotton.

It's beautifully executed. The appliqué is neatly done, but the quilting is outstanding. My mother-in-law didn't quilt. She handed that work over to a woman down the road who quilted like an angel—ten stitches to the inch, absolutely even, each stitch precise. The quilting is a thing of beauty.

The quilt is not.

My mother-in-law made all her quilts the same way: appliqué, in ordinary patterns, but in colors with all the life washed out of them. You can't call them pastel because they've got too much intensity for that. But they are . . . lacking. They are exactly at that stage of color saturation at which boredom is the only possible response.

Her color range was simple: white background (invariably); medium pink (not rose, not fuchsia, not coral, but blameless pink); flat medium or light middle-of-the-road green, no overtones. Sometimes, but not often, blah-yellow. Flat flax blue, medium-light. This quilt is pink and green. It has two shades of each color, one medium, one slightly lighter, each equally lacking in anything much.

Looking at it takes the heart right out of you.

When it is done well, there is in simplicity a plainness that delights. I've been to Sabbathday Lake in Maine, the home of the last living Shakers, and every piece of work I saw there was as plain as could be, but also redolent of joyful practicality and sheer delight in creation. There is curiosity and liveliness and abundance in the Shaker stuff—it sings and dances, in a highly practical way. Yes, to the Shakers, a quilt had to be plain and practical, but that was no reason for it not to play. Not so my mother-in-law's quilts. They sadden me, these pieces. She put such effort into them, and they are so outstandingly insipid.

You could not, however, have turned her from the making of them. She was bound and determined to make us a quilt. It did not occur to her that maybe, if we wanted a quilt, we wanted a queen-sized or at least a generous double quilt. This quilt is barely bigger than a wide single and far too short, but that was the size she made. That was the size she'd inherited, and it never occurred to her to question what she'd inherited. It didn't occur to her to ask us what we'd like in the way of a quilt—whether we'd like something brighter, or more complex. She chose the colors and the pattern and she made the quilt she wanted us to have, and she made it to her own vision. That was, in general, the way she operated. She knew what she wanted us to have. It didn't cross her mind that, perhaps, what she wanted for us was not what we wanted for ourselves.

She was a woman of terrific determination and no imagination. Determination carried her from poverty to respectability. Imagination could have carried her further, if she'd been willing to entertain the idea. She never did.

Her son and I have not been together for a long time now, and she herself is long dead: her life failed to go in the directions she wanted, and she had a bitter and miserable time of it, through her own choice. The quilt she made us sits (as I said) on my closet shelf. It has mysteriously acquired stains that I have no idea what to do about. She made quilts for our two sons: both quilts are much too small, much too insipid; both are appliquéd, both are beautifully quilted. They're folded into my ancestral chest of drawers downstairs. I have no idea what to do with them either. They wait.

MOLLY WOLF *writes essays on God-stuff and has published four collections of essays* (Hiding in Plain Sight; A Place Like Any Other; Angels and Dragons: On Sorrow, God, and Healing; *and* White China: Finding the Divine in the Everyday). *She also coedits the KnitLit series with Linda Roghaar (www.knitlit.com). She lives in Kingston, Ontario, with her two grown sons and three cats.*

MY BOX OF TEARS

- - - - -

GAYLE WAYNE

When I was growing up in the late 1940s and '50s, my mother sewed most of my dresses. Unbeknownst to me, she saved a scrap from each dress she made, and with them, she was making a Victorian crazy quilt to present to me when I was grown.

Tragically, she died from breast cancer when I was sixteen. In the painful process of disposing of her things, I found this unfinished treasure in her sewing room. I learned its story from an aunt who had been sworn to secrecy. The quilt was an agonizing reminder of my mother's love for me and in my raw grief, I couldn't bear to look at it. With teary eyes and hands guided, I am sure, by my mother, I wrapped it carefully in tissue and ribbon, put it in a sturdy box, and stashed it away.

It stayed out of sight for nearly twenty-five years. I always felt its presence in the back of my closet but I never allowed myself to open the box. Whatever would I do with that unfinished quilt?

I married, had my own family, sewed dresses for my daughter, and on her sixteenth birthday, we opened the box together. It still made me cry. So I put it away again. I called it my box of tears.

In 2000, we moved, and that journey required an immense and difficult process of sorting through and downsizing the collected possessions of twenty-five years and two children. The box moved, of course, and was carefully placed in the back reaches of the sewing room in my new home. By this time, I dreamed of retiring, of having time to sew, of buying a fabulous new sewing machine to replace Mother's relic, of learning new skills. A friend and neighbor, Donna, convinced me that I would enjoy learning to quilt and dragged me to a meeting of the Orange Grove Quilters Guild. My mother was in that meeting, in spirit, because the guild's block of the month turned out to be a twelve-inch crazy quilt block, exactly like those in my box of tears.

After the meeting, I rushed home and opened the box. Instead of tears, I had inspiration. I would finish Mother's quilt. Why hadn't I thought of that before?

I found a wonderful lady in a nearby quilt store who looked in my box, ran to the reproduction fabrics, and helped me design the finishing borders and deal with the unfinished embroidery. As we examined the top my mother had made, we found a threaded needle placed in one of the blocks by her hand, tracing her last stitches before she became ill. It had rusted in place. I intend to leave the rust spot and even embellish it.

Wonder of all, my thirty-four-year-old daughter suggested that she help me finish it so it could become a family heirloom, stitched with love by three generations of women. She would even learn to sew and take possession of my old sewing machine, the one that had once belonged to her grandmother.

Now it is no longer a box of tears, this collection of blocks. Instead it is becoming a joyous reminder of how much my mother loved me and how a quilt can become love's own manifestation through the generations.

GAYLE WAYNE *lives, with her growing stash, in Huntington Beach, California, where she enjoys life as a wife, mom, and grandmother of four. Relatively new to quilting, Gayle finds it a fascinating outlet for creativity* and liberating, too, because quilts only have to fit beds and walls, not people! She is working on a book of humorous quilting poetry chronicling her adventures in learning a fine art she naively thought was a simple skill when she began.

BURIED TREASURE

- - - - -

B. LYNN TUBBE

 Studying quilts is almost as fascinating as making quilts. And, as we all know, quilting holds many surprises.

I grew up listening to interesting historical trivia from my dad and watching the women of the family doing needlework. Grandma K's fingers darted in and out of her tatting shuttle, Grandma G's hands swooped around her crochet hook, and Mom knitted magic with her needles. And, of course, all three of them quilted. My earliest memories of handcrafted items were ones of amazement and reverence.

So I felt serious doubt the night Dad talked about buried Civil War quilts. I was studying the Civil War in the fifth grade at the time, and Dad was making his usual dinner comments about my school studies as we passed the mashed potatoes. He explained that when the northerners rumbled toward southern plantations and farms, many valuable items were hidden, buried inside the protection of quilts. I privately doubted that anyone could place treasured quilts, even old and worn ones, under the ground. I finished my meal in silence.

Decades passed and it was my turn to attempt to bring history alive for kids. I combined my love of quilting with historical research of the Civil War period and discovered a wealth of material written for children with quilting as its theme. I stumbled upon fascinating stories about women spies who hid contraband under their hoop skirts, secure in the padded and quilted pockets of their underskirts. I shared research with my students about how quilts might have been used as signaling devices for escaping slaves moving north on the Underground Railroad, and we looked at photographs of intricate quilts made by Civil War soldiers. My students and I brought in quilts, both new and vintage, and proudly hung them in the classroom.

All this served me well in bringing history alive for my eighth-grade students, and it was critical in capturing the attention of the "hormonally impaired." However, when the subject of buried quilts came up, I continued to express my doubts about those stories.

Then one day, my siblings and I gathered in Mom and Dad's garage to watch Dad open three World War II footlockers whose contents hadn't seen the light of day since the 1940s. What treasures tumbled out—canteens, blankets, uniforms, and more than a few items that defied description. Dad, ever the pack rat, had even saved sulfa pills in their original packaging. But something on the bottom of one of the footlockers caught my eye, something oddly pale green, pink, and white.

We carefully reached down and lifted it out. Nearly obliterated by fifty-five years of oil stains, water stains, and rust was a quilt carefully placed to cushion Dad's treasures. It was the right size for a twin bed, had scalloped edging, and was executed in the green and pink shades so beloved by women in the 1930s. The four large, looped designs were edged in green perle cotton appliqué, and I could see that the quilt had been badly faded before being shut up in the dark footlocker for half a century. Even so, the hand quilting was excellent and the perle cotton stitches were precise.

Dad admitted that his mother had used one of her old and damaged quilts to protect her son's war mementos. His treasure had been carefully interred in footlockers rather than in the ground but the end result was the same. A family quilt had made the ultimate sacrifice.

From such simple discoveries is one's vision of history revised. It seemed obvious that if my grandmother had seen fit to use one of her quilts as packaging material, then her foremothers could have done the same during the Civil War.

The following year, my students enjoyed this story about the stained pink and green quilt as part of their Civil War studies. And I plan to display it in tribute to a father who enriched his daughter's love and knowledge of history.

B. LYNN TUBBE *lives in California and is a member of several quilting guilds in the Sierra foothills. She embraces all forms of quilting but is especially fond of art quilts and art-to-wear. Lynn is thrilled that retirement makes it possible to visit shops, shows, conferences, and quilters nationally and internationally.*

THE JOURNEY QUILT

- - - - -

BONNIE REECE

In another life, I worked as a HVAC (heating, ventilating, and air conditioning) mechanic. A woman named Pat was an electrician and worked in the same area as I did. She was a very nice person and well liked by everyone. We had worked together several years when she was diagnosed with breast cancer. She was off work nearly a year undergoing treatment—surgery, chemotherapy, and radiation. When she came back, she'd worked less than six months when the cancer recurred. This time, treatment was not successful and we were told she was terminally ill.

Another woman, a welder, came up with the idea that the women in the crafts should make Pat a "journey quilt." She got the idea from the times when people were leaving their homes and families in the east to journey to the vast, unknown land in the west. Families and friends often made journey quilts to provide warmth and a tangible reminder of the loved ones they were leaving behind.

At that time, there were six women in the crafts—two electricians, a welder, a sheet-metal worker, a maintenance mechanic, and a HVAC mechanic (me). We started meeting at lunchtime and after work to stitch on our blocks. We envisioned a small lap quilt with a block made by each of us and a few other blocks to fill in.

Some of the men found out about our project and wanted to be included. We told them they could contribute blocks but they had to be twelve inches square and made out of cotton fabric. When the blocks started coming in, we knew we had a challenge ahead of us. These men were able to fabricate pipe, wire, and steel to fit exact specifications but the blocks they made were every size from six to twenty inches. And they were made out of all kinds of fabrics, including upholstery vinyl. One guy didn't know how to sew so he glued buttons in the shape of a happy face onto a piece of an old shirt.

It was such an outpouring of love for Pat that we were determined to include everyone's contribution. The irregularly sized blocks were either grouped together or extended with fabric strips to make them the right shape and size. The upholstery vinyl block was stitched down to a fabric piece so it could be included.

It was soon apparent that we were no longer making a small, lap-sized quilt. By the time we were finished, it had turned into a huge banner that was eight by twenty feet. To take a picture of it, we had to have six people hold it up off the ground while a guy took a camera and climbed up onto the roof of a twenty-foot-high building.

I know Pat appreciated the love and caring that that monstrous quilt represented and treasured it until the day she died. It truly was a journey quilt.

BONNIE REECE *started quilting after the death of her first husband. The meditative process of quilting helped her through the grieving process. Now she lives in a RV with her second husband and travels the United States, Canada, and Mexico. They (sewing machine and fabric included) "migrate" to the beach in Loreto, Mexico, every winter.*

ANTIQUE REDWORK

- - - - -

DOROTHY NORTH

 As my friend Ruth was going through her family home in Atlanta after her mother died, she came across a crumpled paper bag of fabric at the back of a drawer. The muslin in the bag was yellowed and musty and from the heavy, irregular folds in it, she could tell the bag hadn't been opened in years. Her first instinct was to toss the whole thing onto the Goodwill pile, but something made her set it aside instead.

The next time we talked, Ruth said her discovery in the paper bag was like nothing she'd ever seen before. The material was all in eight-inch squares and on each a different scene was embroidered in red—an owl, a bunch of grapes, a donkey, a girl in a bonnet. I knew immediately from her description that it was redwork.

Back in the nineteenth century, it was difficult to find embroidery floss in colors that would not fade. Two of the longest lasting were turkey red and indigo blue. Traditionally, redwork is embroidered in either a running or stem stitch done in this turkey red floss. The images made in redwork are usually simple line drawings of children, fruit, birds, or other domestic subjects. Sometimes redwork was used to commemorate a special event such as a centennial or a fair.

My own quilting has focused mostly on machine piecing; I love to cut and piece fabric. But as a girl, I'd learned to embroider and although I've long ago outgrown the simple cross-stitch patterns of my youth, I still have happy memories of sitting for hours surrounded by skeins of embroidery floss as I compared shades, trying out one color next to another and practicing new stitches. Embroidery was probably my first step on the road to becoming a quilter and I had thought about trying my hand at redwork.

Ruth packed up the squares and shipped them from Atlanta to my home near San Francisco. When I opened the package, my heart sank because they were even more soiled than I had imagined. But with some help from my quilt teacher, Julie, they cleaned up beautifully after I soaked them in a brew of grated Fels-Naptha soap in a pot of hot water. Once they were rinsed, dried, and pressed, they looked almost new.

The squares were sewn together into rows two blocks wide and eight long, apparently with the plan of making a bed-sized quilt with the redwork set around a solid center. The machine-stitched seams between the blocks were outlined in a double feather stitch. Ruth was hoping I could make a wall hanging for her law office in Atlanta so I set out to rearrange the blocks for that purpose. This meant, of course, that I had to take out some of the feather-stitched embroidery and the machine stitching.

The embroidery was easy enough to pick out, but the tiny machine stitches were as tight as rivets. The point of my seam ripper was too big to release some of the seams so I had to pick out the stitches with a needle.

After I got the squares rearranged and sewn into a rectangle, I started to think about the feather stitching. About half of the original stitching remained on top of the machine variety. That's when I noticed it wasn't all done in the same shade of red. Some of it was turkey red, some of it was bright red. I went to the shelf in my closet where I keep a supply of embroidery threads I bought on a trip to Yugoslavia in 1971. I picked through the dozens of slender cardboard boxes with their Serbian writing, wondering what I'd been thinking of when I bought this lifetime supply of embroidery thread. But it had been hard to resist because the colors were so rich and saturated. I stopped for a moment to lay a skein of turquoise next to the blue; the combination reminded me of the sea on the Adriatic coast. As it turned out, it was lucky that I had bought so much, because I found a medium red that worked well with the reds already in the blocks.

I threaded a number eight embroidery needle and began to practice the double feather stitch. But try as I could, my stitches just didn't match the ones in the redwork. Then I began to notice some inconsistencies in the original. I studied the back of the work and saw that some of the stitching was tight and exact, straddling the machine-stitched seams perfectly. Other rows seemed more haphazard and casual, sometimes twisting the flat folds of the muslin, other times tacking the fabric down, sometimes missing it entirely. With a growing sense of anxiety, I began to apply my own version of the double feather stitch to the joints between the blocks.

In the meantime, Ruth had gone to visit her mother's only remaining sister. Her aunt vaguely remembered the redwork though she didn't know that's what it was called. She also remembered a story that it had been done by her own grandmother Lillian Kent Barrington and her great aunt, Lillian's sister, Angie Kent, where they lived in the Derry/Londonderry area of New Hampshire. Doing some rough calculations, they figured the redwork had been done somewhere between 1910 and 1920.

Ruth called to tell me the news. That explained the two types of stitches. Now as I embroidered, I imagined the two sisters talking while they sat and stitched through the cold winters and humid summers of New Hampshire. I wondered if these different stitches were evidence of different personalities in the sisters. One, perhaps, was carefree and easygoing, and hadn't minded that the back of her work was untidy. Maybe she thought to herself, Who will ever notice? The other sister—maybe the older one, the taskmistress—may have thought, It does matter how the stitches look from the back. Maybe it was this same sister who machine stitched the squares together with those tiny stitches. She was sewing for keeps.

Did they talk about these things? Were their different styles a source of tension or a source of amusement to them? Or was this something so ingrained in them from their childhoods that they weren't even conscious of it? I thought about these things as I stitched. I wondered what the New Hampshire sisters would have thought if, as they sat stitching, someone had told them that many years later, a woman unrelated to them, living across the country in California, would finish their work for their great-granddaughter and great-great-niece. I saw their startled faces lift from the sewing in their laps at this notion.

I put the work up on my design wall. It was getting closer but the sisters' feather stitching was more square, and mine more, well, feathered. I just couldn't match theirs. Then it dawned on me. It wasn't supposed to match. Two pairs of hands began the redwork. Now eighty or so years later, a third pair of hands— my hands—were taking up the work to get this project out of the drawer and on the wall to be admired. This third style of feather stitch was my own signature on the redwork. Now I was excited. Now the work started to move quickly.

I found a fabric with small white flowers on a turkey-red background that was perfect for the binding. I constructed the back by making pinwheels from the red floral print, some muslin, and a solid red fabric. I added a thin cotton batting and tied the quilt with more of the red embroidery floss. Ruth and I composed a legend for the quilt, detailing as much as she could learn about Lillian and Angie, and the trail of ownership of the quilt down through the generations to Ruth's mother and now to Ruth. We included the fact that we had met in law school in San Francisco and had been friends for over thirty years. Ruth painted a wall in her office and waited for the FedEx truck to return her quilt to Atlanta, where it now hangs.

The restoration of Ruth's family redwork took a lot longer than I expected but it was worth it. Out of it, in addition to enriching my friendship with Ruth, I feel as though I got a second trip to Yugoslavia and met two quilting sisters from New Hampshire. Who says quilting is just a hobby?

DOROTHY NORTH's *poetry and prose have appeared in various publications including* Poet Lore, Hotel Amerika, *and* Knit Lit the Third. *She lives near San Francisco, works as an attorney specializing in workmen's compensation, and is a member of the Peninsula Quilters Guild of San Mateo, California.*

SCRAPPING WITH ELIJAH

- - - - -

CHERRY MORGENSTEIN RACUSIN

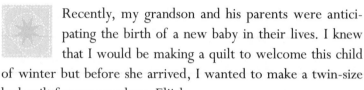 Recently, my grandson and his parents were anticipating the birth of a new baby in their lives. I knew that I would be making a quilt to welcome this child of winter but before she arrived, I wanted to make a twin-size bed quilt for my grandson, Elijah.

At five years old, Elijah is, among other things, a sports guy—a daredevil on my furniture, a jaguar on skis, a darting fish on a sled. At preschool, he practices snowboarding by standing on a plastic sled and descending the playground's gentle slope. He has aspirations to go from ice skating with a crate (to steady him as he learns) to joining an ice hockey team, and he's had many an exciting game during our dramatic playtimes together.

I asked Elijah to help me pick out the fabrics for his quilt. We went to my favorite local quilt shop, the Quilter's Courtyard, an oasis of colors and textures in the midst of our winter's monochromatic landscape. I lingered at the batiks until he called me over to see the shelf he'd found of sports-theme fabrics. There were hockey players and flying pucks on a blue background; surfers, snowboarders, skiers, and bikers against a blue and white sky; footballs on blue ground; soccer balls and stars blinking energy on every square inch. I piled up the bolts. Then Elijah found a purple constellation fabric and a marbled print in purple and white that resembled the surface of water. We added those to my pile as well as multicolored, striped lizards moving on a rich black ground.

"Is that it?" I asked. He nodded.

Elijah may have been satisfied but I was boggled. For years, I'd made patchwork pieces that sang in soft harmonies with one another. In fact, I've made only one big, noisy quilt and that one's a tribute to my surprise at having hot flashes light me up when I reached menopause. It's full of hot and intense colors like apricot, blood orange, lemon, azure, scarlet, and plum that shimmy and dance with startled bursts of color, a shouted-out gospel song of connecting blocks and background. But even that quilt hadn't prepared me for Elijah's choices.

As I walked toward the counter under the weight of seven bolts of fabric, I thought about my quilt books. Which one of them would hold the key to turning this disparate collection of stick-hitting, sliding, bouncing, rolling, crawling, and airborne fabrics into something resembling an integrated patchwork?

The very first quilt book I ever bought, over thirty years ago, was Ruby McKim's classic *101 Patchwork Patterns*. I still have, tucked among its pages, the cardboard templates I cut out for Shoofly, Wild Goose Chase, and Road to Oklahoma that I used for long-ago quilts I made for my children when they were very young. Since then, my library has grown to sixty volumes, including how-tos and purely inspirational art quilt books.

In addition to using books for patterns, hints, and cutting methods, I've learned to create designs using my own templates. Each summer I go to the Vermont Quilt Festival to take workshops with professional quiltmakers. They have nurtured my ability to take risks and my desire for meaningful play, processes I supported in my students when I was a preschool teacher. But standing in the shop looking at those lively fabrics, I drew a blank. What was I going to do with them?

Beth, who owned the quilt shop, smiled encouragement when I placed my dismay on top of the fabric bolts. "Well, that is quite a selection," she agreed. "Why don't you try a Scrappie quilt? That would be the way to go."

I tried to be enthusiastic in response. I wanted to believe she had just given me the key I was searching for in my mind's eye as I mentally flipped through the pages of my remembered library.

I'd made a Scrappie quilt once before. In fact, it was the first quilt I'd ever made. The Scrappie, or Scrap, quilt is true to its name. It's made up of many fabric pieces, the more the better—solids, small prints, large ones, patterned prints—all in various hues and shades. It's a great way to use both leftover fabric and fabrics you just can't believe you ever bought. For that first Scrappie quilt, I'd chosen calico prints, mostly small florals, of yellow, green, and blue with an occasional pink sprinkled throughout. It did not have the pictures or the range of colors facing me.

I washed and ironed Elijah's selections and looked through books for ideas. I wanted the structure of a pattern to give underlying form to the fabrics, to keep the action from escaping, and to prevent the quilt from being visually chaotic and dizzying. I wanted the rows set on the diagonal to give the movement coherence. I finally found a Scrappie pattern using squares, both patched and whole cloth. I cut the patch pieces freely, with no templates, keeping the pictures intact. The result was that no completed square looked like any other save for the fabrics used. The whole cloth squares, including a black on deep blue that I found in my stash, alternated with those patchwork squares. Whole cloth triangles filled in the edges.

I've discovered that quiltmaking is a great motivation for doing housework. I vacuumed and mopped the front room of my house, the only one with enough empty space to accommodate the quilt during its creation. Then I lay the pieces on the clean floor to construct this jigsaw puzzle without a picture.

I sound as if I were in more control of that process than I was, and that it proceeded in a calm, linear fashion. But I felt sure of only the whole cloth squares, which I placed with enough space in between for the alternating patched blocks. That still left a lot of room for discovery, surprise, and change as I tried to compose a whole design from many small ones. Then I discovered I didn't have enough fabric and went to buy more. To all of Elijah's picks, I added a length of basketballs on a grid of black and blue. Then I had to rearrange the pieces throughout the design in order to integrate this new sport motif into the assortment.

As I crouched around the growing quilt, bending and stretching to place the inner pieces, I was constantly shooing away my two large cats, who, ever curious, are always on the lookout for comfortable squatters' quarters in the midst of my work. I chased them off the design only to have them scatter pieces as they leapt up and away. In defense, I pinned the pieces together, unpinning them as I made changes. It was a tedious process, but it kept my sanity intact and enabled me to share the emerging quilt with my cats.

As I constructed the quilt top, I stopped, walked upstairs, looked over the banister, and saw the progress I was making. It worked. The prints formed visual connections as if there were tiny hockey, football, soccer, and basketball games taking place simultaneously with surfers, boarders, and bikers weaving throughout. And underfoot, everywhere, moved all those lizards.

I finished the patchwork top and added borders in coordinating fabric to complete the necessary width and length. I tied the three layers together in each block's corners. There are quiltmakers who believe that quilts should be stitched, preferably by hand, and not just tied. I admire those people who can not only complete a patchwork top but quilt it and live, with their faculties intact, to repeat the process. I am not one of those people. I tried, once, to machine quilt and ended up with an inadvertent, wrinkled, ungainly trapunto effect. I tried hand quilting, bought an instruction book, and even took a class to learn to sew proper stitches. Depending on my mood when I picked up the work, my stitches were long or tiny, loose or tight but never consistent for any length of time or line. I couldn't figure out designs and stitching in the ditch seemed like a pointless bore. Instead of being meditative, quilting made me so tense that I stopped—and have happily tied my quilts ever since.

Once Elijah's quilt was tied, I bound the edges, washed it, and brought it on my next visit to my family. Elijah unpacked it and immediately tried it out, lying beneath it so the flannel back was soft against his skin. If I had had a lot of trials and doubts about this quilt, it was apparent that Elijah did not share them for he declared our collaborative quilt a total success.

For decades, CHERRY MORGENSTEIN RACUSIN *worked with children as a preschool teacher and with refugees in the Burlington, Vermont, area, where she lived. She had been quilting for well over thirty years when she died in October 2006. With each project, Cherry aimed to expand her vision and learn new skills. She created quilts with preschoolers and helped families make commemorative quilts for the Names Project.*

AUNTIE LINDA'S QUILTING LESSON

- - - - -

GINNY LEVIN

I wasn't raised in a family that valued handcrafts much. My mother is still the best cook I've ever known, and I consider that her creative outlet. But her only nod in the direction of handcrafts is painting. No, I don't mean watercolors or oils. I mean painting, as on houses and furniture. All the tables and chairs in our ancestral home have at least ten coats of paint on them, each layer reflecting one of my mother's color phases from the past. Recently, when one of my brothers stripped an old bench that held a featured position in our hallway for years, it was like an archaeological dig, with each layer of removed paint representing a different part of our growing up—the harvest gold period, the turquoise and tan experiment, the chilling black-and-white art deco era. Mom wielded a mean paintbrush and her meatballs were famous all over town, but pick up a needle and thread? No way.

Now to be fair to both sides of my parents' marital equation, my father was actually seen sewing once and to hear him tell the story, you'd think that that event had an immediate impact on my DNA. But I swear I wasn't even in the room when he mended my youngest brother's teddy bear with a needle he wheedled from our next-door neighbor, Lillian. In fact, I've always suspected that it was really Lillian who did the sewing.

I never realized my family had a handcraft deficit until I got my first Barbie doll. I was ten at the time, a little late to be acquiring that plastic role model of all things good and girlie (according to the TV ads anyway). But before that, I'd been busy playing Wiffle ball with the boys in the neighborhood and laying pennies on the railroad tracks for the trains to flatten. Important stuff, you know?

I think my mother had some concerns about my lack of playtime with my female friends and thought that a doll just might tip me over the edge. As it turns out, she was right but not in the way she'd planned.

My best friend in school was Charlotte Palmer. I felt she was eminently qualified for this lofty position in my life because her mother made the most delicious gingersnaps in the world, the best tobogganing hill in the neighborhood was in the Palmers' backyard, and Charlotte was an experienced Barbie owner. So on the day after my tenth birthday, I traipsed off to Charlotte's house with my plastic Barbie maiden tucked under my arm, wondering what kind of games you played with these things.

When I got to the Palmers', I found Charlotte and her mother (I think her name was Lois) both in this room I'd never seemed to notice before. I walked in and it was as if a rainbow had exploded in there. I don't think I'd ever seen so much color in one place at one time. There were reds of all shades from mauve to scarlet, pale lemon yellows, prints with paisleys small and large, blues like the sky, and a slash of orange or two. Charlotte was sitting right in the middle of it all, clutching a Barbie doll while her mother held up a scrap of shiny, pale green fabric with tiny white flowers all over it.

"Don't you think this would make a great dress for Barbie?" Charlotte shrieked when she saw me.

I was too color-stunned to do much more than nod. "Sure, yeah," I said.

"You can sew a dress for your Barbie, too," Mrs. Palmer said, "if you like."

Coming on top of seeing all that fabric scattered about the room, Mrs. Palmer's words were too much for me to take in. "Sew?" I asked. "You sew clothes? Are you allowed to do that for Barbies?"

Mrs. Palmer's face did this really funny dance for a couple of minutes after I said that. She murmured something that sounded like "you poor dear" but there was so much giggle in her words, it was hard to tell. I realize now that she was hovering somewhere between mild shock, pity, and laughter while I stood there feeling foolish. Fortunately, Charlotte didn't seem to notice her mother's struggle. Instead, she grabbed my hand and dragged me over to a bureau festooned with fabric.

"This is all mine," she said with a great deal of pride. "Mom and her friends save their scraps for me. We can share."

I have to give Charlotte and her mother a great deal of credit for the patience they had with someone who'd never even seen a sewing needle before. Mrs. Palmer showed me how to poke that pesky thread through that little hole ("That's right, keep the tongue out to the side") and Charlotte taught me a trick to knot the end without fussing over it. Then they both took turns soothing my frustrations while I tried to maneuver that pointed metal thing in a straight line through a piece of fabric in order to make a skirt for my Barbie.

Over the next few months, that sewing room became my treasure cave, and I swear no pirate ever coveted doubloons as much as I coveted every little piece of fabric that Charlotte or her mother would share with me. I'd spend hours when I was supposed to be sleeping, moving a small collection of scraps—my first stash—around on my bedroom floor to make designs that looked like flowers or snakes or a mass of kites on a windy day.

But it all ended quite suddenly when Charlotte's father got

transferred to some place I'd never heard of before and the Palmers moved away.

I kept Charlotte's parting gift of scraps in a box under my bed, untouched, until I threw it away the last time I cleaned my room before I headed off to college. I told myself that it was the color bug that had bitten me—something I guess I share with my mother—not the sewing bug.

And that was true for the next twenty or so years until one day, at a town planning meeting of all places, I spotted a woman quilting a block that she later told me was part of a Christmas present. If you're a quilter, you can imagine that she needed no prompting to drag out all the other blocks she'd finished from the depths of this capacious bag at her feet. I was color-stunned all over again.

"Where did you learn to do this?" I asked her.

"Oh, here and there, some things from my mother, some from friends, and I took a couple of classes," she said.

"Classes? Where?"

She mentioned the name of a quilt shop located some thirty miles away. "Make sure you take a beginner's class," she said.

I couldn't wait to get home, couldn't wait to find the quilt shop's number, and couldn't wait to sign up for their next class in basic quilting. "I don't sew at all," I said before I handed over my credit-card number to the shop's owner. "Are you sure I'll be able to do this?"

"Oh, no problem. Linda is an excellent teacher," the voice on the other end reassured me. "And we have a machine here that you can use."

I should have been tipped off by the word "machine" but I was so giddy, I don't think I clearly heard what she said.

A few days passed and I received a confirmation of my class reservation in the mail along with a list of supplies that I needed to bring with me. It was a long list, especially for someone who did not sew at all—pins (preferably glass headed), rotary cutter (with extra blades, recommended), fabrics in different shades of two colors, cutting matt, tape measure, drafting pencil, finger grips (recommended but not required), quilting ruler, seam ripper, scissors, and a steam iron. I gasped when I read the words "scissors, and a steam iron" because they were the only things on the list that I recognized.

If the woman at that town meeting hadn't made it look so easy, I would have quit right there. But I was getting stubborn. I called the shop again but before I could finish saying "what's a rotary cutter?" the woman on the other end of the line reassured me again.

"We have everything you need right here. Just plan to come a half hour early and we'll get you all set up," she said.

So I did, and she was wonderful, patiently explaining how each implement was used and generously offering to let me use some of the store's supplies. She even directed me toward the fat quarter sales table and selected fabric for me. As I waited for the other students and the teacher to arrive, I browsed the store's book selection, lingering over a thick volume that promised to teach a novice all she needed to know to make a quilt.

"Oh, you won't need that," the storekeeper told me. "This class will teach you all the basics."

But once the introductions were over, the class moved in a decidedly downhill direction. To me, a bobbin was what a "red, red robin" did in a song. I couldn't keep my ruler from sliding across my fabric no matter how hard I tried to keep it in place. The term "right side down" made no sense to me whatsoever, and somehow, two of my right-angle triangles ended up oblique. Don't ask.

I've been quilting for almost ten years now, and with all the wisdom I've gained over the past decade, I now realize that that teacher's notion of what constituted a class for beginning quilters bore no resemblance to my need. I would have been ecstatic if I'd conquered the mechanics of threading a sewing machine and cutting out squares for a simple Nine Patch. But Miss Roberts (as she liked to be called, can you imagine?) insisted on teaching us Sawtooth, a pattern consisting of twenty-eight triangles of two different sizes combined with five squares.

After six hours of cutting and breaking thread and frustration, I had made myself a pile of rather expensive scraps. Somehow, Miss Roberts didn't notice. She spent the last hour of class time regaling us with stories about the latest addition to her family, a nephew named Joshua, who, she assured us, was as "cute as his daddy." Miss Roberts felt especially keen that day because she'd just finished making the baby quilt that everyone in her family had come to expect from "Auntie Linda." And what was even better, she had the quilt with her because she was going to visit Joshua and his proud family on her way home from teaching our "basic quilting" class.

By this time, I'd quietly made my way toward the back of the room, collecting my fabric and notions with a vow to never, ever touch a needle or thread again. Just then, one of the other students begged Miss Roberts to show us her quilt. I am so glad I didn't miss it.

Beaming, the proud aunt cleared a place on a worktable to display her finished baby bed covering. With a sweeping glance around the room, she slid it out of its plastic-bag sheath and spread it out for all to see.

I'm sure there were other colors in that quilt but I swear, the only one I remember is the yellow. This was not some dainty, lemon-custard color. Nor did it have the self-confident tone of a sunflower. Nope, this was the loudest screaming yellow you can imagine. A satellite flying overhead could have used this yellow as a homing beacon. Aliens on a distant planet probably figured they'd found another star when Linda spread out this quilt.

My jaw dropped. The top of Joshua's gift didn't seem to be exactly the same size as its back and the quilt was lumpy in places where it should have been smooth. But that yellow just overwhelmed all other considerations. I hoped that poor Joshua's parents would have the good sense to hide that thing in a closet as soon as Aunt Linda was out the door.

But for this beginning quilter, it was the best part of the lesson. Suddenly, seeing that finished quilt with its garish color selection and uneven fit made sewing more accessible to me. With a big grin nearly splitting my face in half, I marched myself out of that classroom, over to the store's bookshelf, and picked up that volume on basic quilting. I haven't stopped since.

GINNY LEVIN *lives with her partner, Clark, in a small town in upstate New York. She's a member of two guilds, and when she was out of the room recently, the members of one of them elected her their president. She reports that she does use the occasional patch of yellow in a quilt and never fails to think of Miss Roberts when she does. Once in a while, she gets asked to teach classes in the basics of quilting and always starts her students off with Nine Patch.*

COINCIDENCE 1.0

LAURA A. BARNETT

My cousin Hoy-Ann and I are the daughters of twin sisters. Over the years, we've witnessed what's known as the "twin phenomenon"—the regularly recurring coincidence—many times. For example, our mothers often wear the same style and/or colors at holiday get-togethers and they share a favorite pastime—shopping excursions. One birthday, they even sent an identical Hallmark card to each other.

While many traditions or hobbies are handed down from one generation to the next, Hoy-Ann and I never expected this twin phenomenon to extend to us—until we both wanted to take a class from the same quilt shop in Mountain View, California. Hoy-Ann and I live approximately one and a half hours from each other and Mountain View is a great place to meet in the middle. After discussing what to take, we decided on a sampler class, figuring it was a wonderful opportunity to learn quilt basics and visit with each other at the same time.

In all of our planning, the topic of what fabric theme or colors we were going to purchase never came up. As far as we knew, the only coincidence about taking this class together was that we had both procrastinated and needed to buy fabric quickly before it started. The ladies in my quilt shop must have known I was a desperate woman when I purchased yards and yards of fabric. But it simply had to be done because I didn't have enough fabric in my stash for a true sampler quilt!

A few days later when Hoy-Ann and I saw each other at our first class meeting, we were shocked to find out that each of us had chosen a patriotic theme, that we were the only ones in the class to have placed our neatly pressed fabric on hangers, and that we had even chosen an identical fabric. None of the other students had duplicated anything at all and they were as amazed at the coincidence as Hoy-Ann and I were.

And yes, both of our quilts are still works in progress.

LAURA A. BARNETT *lives on the central coast of California in Santa Cruz County and has been a member of the Pajaro Valley Quilt Association since 2000. She's been quilting since 1994 and is inspired by all of the talented members of her guild. Her unfinished quilt list is longer than her wish list!*

AN UNORTHODOX QUILTER

and How She Grew

- - - - -

MARCIA BURCH

My mother loved to sew. She mended whatever needed mending, made nightgowns for her newborn grand-children, dresses and Barbie clothes for the girls as they grew, pajamas for the boys, and curtains for our houses. But sewing was not in my repertoire. In fact, I never went to visit her without a pile of things that needed mending or a list of things that needed making.

Needless to say, all of Mom's activities produced a lot of left-over material and it all needed a home when she left this life. So I vowed to overcome my aversion to needle and thread and packed up Mom's treasures to take home, promising myself that I would make patchwork quilts for her grandchildren as a way to honor and preserve her memory.

But it was difficult for me to put that intention into action— you know what road is paved with good intentions. Every time I looked at that material and contemplated making some quilts, the thought of cutting precise little pieces and putting them to-gether in intricate patterns deterred me from ever starting.

Then one day I went to a friend's house when she was having a yard sale. My friend is a seamstress, just like my mother was. Among the "this and that" of the sale, I found some Waverly fabric sample books. My friend remarked that they were a great source of material for "crazy quilts." When I looked puzzled, she showed me the one she had made and explained how to put one together.

A crazy quilt block starts with a twelve-inch square of muslin to which one sews two pieces of material in the middle and then you add odd-sized scraps until the square is covered. There are no precise cuttings or piecing and the squares grow like Topsy. This was just the ticket for me and my mother's scraps.

It took awhile but over time, I made a crazy quilt from Mom's scraps for each one of her grandchildren. And wonder of wonders, I enjoyed the process and was pleased with the results. Every time I sat at the sewing machine to work on a quilt, I thought about her and how surprised and pleased she would be to see me there and I hoped that somehow she knew.

But my quilting adventures weren't done, because, you see, I had bought those fabric sample books. This was not crazy quilt material, however. Here were these uniformly shaped pieces— why not use them "as is" by sewing them in rows then joining the results with coordinating strips of material? I acquired some more discarded sample books from friends who owned a fabric store and I was soon elbow deep in patchwork.

Then a friend bought the book *Make a Quilt in a Day: Log Cabin Pattern* and attended a workshop on the process. Inspired by her success, I bought the book and more material and with my friend's guidance, made my first Log Cabin quilt for my first grandchild.

I found I loved the Log Cabin pattern for the same reason I enjoyed crazy quilting and patchwork—it's simple and stream-lined. To this day, all my quilts are machine sewn and tied, nothing fancy, and I won't win any prizes at craft fairs. But my efforts are warming and comforting for the people who sleep under them. Some have become the beloved "binnies" for children who cannot go to bed without them. In fact, one of my granddaughter's cousins, who was nine at the time, brought me her quilt in tatters to ask if I could mend it. My mother would have been so proud. I fixed the top and re-bound it to a back of the same ma-

terial as the original. I'm told the little one cried tears of joy
when she saw it and sleeps with it still.

Now that's what I call success.

MARCIA BURCH *lives in New Hampshire, but her heart belongs to her
native Vermont. The quilting hobby has provided experiences to share with
friends like shopping trips and "tying bees." When she was the librarian in
a middle school, she provided the impetus for an activity that became a
tradition—making quilts for new babies of faculty members.*

I DIDN'T GROW UP IN
A SEWING HOUSEHOLD

- - - - -

DENISE CAWLEY

In my house growing up, the Kenmore sewing machine existed only as a piece of furniture to hold the clothes to be mended and the clothes to be ironed until we either grew out of them or they grew out of style. I remember once my mother tried to make me a tooth-fairy pillow using that machine and it took her two days of swearing at and fighting with the bobbin to complete the task. The tooth-fairy's arrival had to be postponed for the pillow. I don't recall the Kenmore being used much after that.

The only person I knew who sewed—let alone quilted—was my Aunt Ann (names changed to protect the embarrassed). While my childhood eyes admired the fact that she could sew, things from her rarely fit and they were often in colors I didn't like. When I was about eighteen, Aunt Ann learned to quilt. Typical of everything she did, her hand quilting stitches were tiny and precise so it was such a shame to me that the quilts she made were ugly, often made from fabric purchased at stores with more than one location.

I grew up in Michigan but at eighteen, I moved to Brooklyn to attend school in Greenwich Village, a big change for me. I diligently practiced drawing and design and often did fifty hours or more of homework a week. I took in lots of art shows and knew how to get into any cultural event without spending more than a few dollars. I worked cleaning houses to make ends meet.

I was always told you had to stay ten years—even ten years past graduation—in order to "make it" in New York as an artist. But in 1993, at Parsons School of Design, the department of my college major fell apart. My mom was ill, money was in short supply, and I was depressed. I had to leave Parsons. I had to leave New York without having stayed long enough to become an artist. I had to go home. I felt like a failure.

Later on, the universe brought me just where I was supposed to be and I finished my degree at a women's college in Wisconsin. During that time, I fell in love with batik as well as hand dyeing for paper and fabrics. I created artist's books. I was interested in series, symbols, and stories. I often created huge wall hangings out of silk but I had no idea how to even sew a seam around the edges. In my mind, sewing was an ancient skill that was no longer necessary in our modern age.

My interest in fiber art continued to grow after I graduated but all of my pieces remained unsewn. I mounted fabric on canvas stretchers. I altered found-object textiles like tablecloths, which were already sewn together and had finished edges. It didn't even occur to me to learn how to sew.

In 1997, I was working in a gallery and was about to leave to start a "real" job after college graduation. The gallery begged me to stay on a little longer and help with a big quilt show that was coming to town. Thoughts of *Little House on the Prairie* came to mind so I was shocked when the show that came was Nancy Crow's Improvisational Quilts from the Smithsonian's Renwick Gallery.

Bold colors, hand-dyed fabrics, striking compositions, contemporary art, and themes I could relate to were stitched throughout those quilts. I had no idea quilting could be so vibrant, interesting, and for me, life changing. Here was a woman who lived in the Midwest—like me. She hand dyed fabrics—like me. She was a successful artist and didn't live in New York City. I felt like a loser when I left New York, but here was this woman who was an international success and she lived on a farm in Ohio. I was so enthralled by that show it filled my dreams nightly.

During the next few years I attempted to learn to sew. I started looking at quilts. I reexamined all the *FiberArts* magazines I had drooled over. I imagined how I could enhance my art if I learned to not just sew but quilt. I fell in love with the work of Ellen Anne Eddy. But when I showed veteran quilters and stitchers my ideas for the pieces I wanted to learn to quilt, I was told, "It will take years and years to learn that and you will need a very expensive sewing machine." Frequently I was told, "You will never be able to do that." But my passion and desire to learn were too strong to be put off by these negative assessments. I continued to talk to every person I knew who quilted. I even got close with my Aunt Ann and pressed her to tell me everything she knew about quilting.

I drove to Michigan, to my mother's house, and removed the ironing and mending piles from the top of the Kenmore sewing machine. I got it overhauled and then stared at it in wonder. I didn't know how to work it. My mother couldn't show me how to use it, because she had forgotten by then. Finally, I talked a friend's mom into coming over and showing me how to turn the machine on. She sat with me for about an hour and taught me how to wind bobbins and thread the machine. I showed her Ellen Anne Eddy's book and she said that that was done by dropping the feed dogs. "Where are those?" I asked. To my delight she showed me.

I started practicing whenever I could. I read every book I found on quilting. I started taking quilting classes. I wanted to ground myself in the basics of quilting just like I had grounded myself in the basics of art in art school by learning disciplines like drawing, color, figure drawing, and art history. At quilt stores I either met people who were amazed by what I was trying to do with my sewing machine or people who rejected me. There was even one woman who told me not to shop in her store anymore. I really wanted to learn what these people knew but my quilts were labeled "art," not quilts, and that wasn't always favored.

Thankfully, Nancy Crow's quilts had stirred up so much passion in me that I didn't stop trying to connect with other quilters until I found places where I was welcomed. As people discovered my art knowledge, I was asked to teach color theory at local stores. Then I finally quit that real job to do my art and teach full-time.

Today, my art quilts, or "quilted paintings," as I like to call them, show in galleries, juried museum exhibits, and are in collections in private homes and businesses. I am a master of thread. I consider what I do to be drawing with thread. I paint with fabric using commercial materials bought at stores with just one location or with my own hand-dyed fabrics. My passion for teaching started in college when I was a teaching assistant, continued in corporate America, and thrives today in my lectures and workshops. My nontraditional way of learning to quilt allows me to give others the sense that they can control their own creative passion.

Every time I teach or lecture, I come across people who tell me they will never be able to quilt like I do. They give soliloquies about how they cannot draw, they are not creative, and all they can do is follow a pattern. Now I'm the one who says, "You can learn to draw and I can teach you. You are creative and I can prove it." I love helping others wake up their creativity. I teach color confidence, thread drawing, fabric dyeing, complex cloth, and more. I know my methods work because of what students produce and what they say after studying with me. They tell me, "You are a source of inspiration—a shot in the arm." Or they write, "Your class always challenges me to go to a higher level. The right brain needed a kick." These are the same students who had previously listened to the quilt police, who shut down their creativity. I aim to help them quiet the critics and create from their soul.

A year ago, I traveled to Nancy Crow's barn to study with Jane Dunnewold. Because it was Nancy Crow who started this quilting passion in me, it felt like a full-circle experience to travel to her home in Ohio. I believe I am living the life I was called to live, combining all of my talents and interests into my quilting passion.

DENISE CAWLEY *is a fiber artist showing her work in galleries and museums. Her aim is to bring out untapped creativity and potential in individuals through her lectures and workshops at guilds and museums. To find out more about her company, Pizzazz Studios, to view her quilts, shop at her online store, or learn about her lectures and workshops, visit www.pizzazzstudios.com.*

DIFFERENT IDEAS

- - - - -

LYNN HEATH

I started quilting because quilts don't talk back.

It was my great fortune to have three children, and I loved to sew for them. First came my boys, who cared little about clothes and would wear any sweet little thing I put on them. I made one-piece suits for them as babies, then overalls, shorts, and T-shirts. Each season I bought fabrics in a variety of mix-and-match colors—rugged fabrics and primary colors suitable for my all-American boys. The son who couldn't keep his pants up wore overalls with fire engines, dinosaurs, illustrations from his favorite books. One pair was the color of his deep brown eyes with a big candy kiss in silver on the front. On the paper streamer coming out of it, I embroidered, "This kiss is for you." Oh, they were adorable, cherubs with curls, one light and one dark.

When my daughter was born, I went nuts with possibility, as did everyone else. In fact, I once counted fifteen variations on pink rosebuds among her dresses, blankets, booties, and bonnets. She was going to be my own doll to dress and cuddle!

Catherine, however, had different ideas, and she let me know about them early. From the time she learned to undress—long before she learned to talk—she made it clear that she was only going to wear attire of her own choice. She loved clothes as much as I did, but she and I had serious disagreements on style. Our family album is full of her fashion statements: a sundress paired with thigh-high rubber boots, a square of fabric pinned to her underwear in six places, nine stamps artfully glued to her otherwise naked body. One picture reveals her solution to the dilemma of which shorts to wear—just pile on three extra pairs, one on each arm and one on her head. In another photo, she is outside on a snowy day, dressed in a diaper and a quilt. One of her first sentences was, "It's not so cold!" as she shed her clothes on a brisk fall day.

Slow to learn, I continued to sew cunning outfits for her with appliqués and quilted designs—baby birds in a nest, clowns, whole carousels, four dolls enjoying a picnic! One Christmas dress has not only Santa in a sleigh full of toys pulled by three reindeer, but also a house below with a little girl looking out the attic window. There are candles in the upstairs windows, as well as a decorated Christmas tree in the living room. When you open the door (wreath-adorned), there's a fireplace hung with stockings, cookies, and juice for Santa, carrots for the reindeer, more candles on the mantle. She looked at it and said, "You know what would be really neat? If the little girl looking out the window was wearing a dress with a pocket that had a house with a little girl looking out the window."

"Time for bed," I cheerfully replied.

I made matching outfits for her dolls. I let her choose fabrics, patterns, colors. For one dress, she directed the placement of each bead and sequin. Excited, she told me, "I love this dress! I'm going to wear it every . . . once in a while." She knew her limitations, her inability to commit. And she knew me, too. Even in preschool, she knew her behavior was ungrateful and maddening. A friend reported one day that Catherine responded to a compliment on a hand-knitted sweater with the comment, "Yes, it's very pretty, and I know my mother worked very hard on it, but actually, I don't care for it that much." Devil child!

I gave away some of her clothes to children I hoped would appreciate them, an ill-disguised and unsuccessful attempt to induce guilt. I put others in the attic for the next generation. Finally, I had to face the reality that sewing for my daughter would not be a happy experience for either of us.

And so I turned my energy to quilts. I had made several baby quilts for friends by this time and had been sewing clothes for twenty-five years, so I had a sizable stash of fabrics. I had always haunted fabric outlets and sales, buying fabrics to use at some later date. I had organized a neat little box of index cards with swatches, yardage, and intentions. I would soon learn that if you can still inventory your fabric, you don't have enough of it.

One of my first quilts was simple pinwheels made from all the corduroys from Catherine's overalls. It's lovely and cuddly, but it's not a very good quilt. Corduroy frays easily, and the quilt was falling apart even before I finished the top. I used a sheet as backing and a puffy polyester batting and then tied it. We decided to use it till it fell apart and to have no regrets when it did. Fifteen years later, it's still a good choice on a cold winter's night.

The woodwork in Catherine's room was painted the color of raspberry sherbet, a disastrous choice I decided to offset with a quilt. I gathered about 150 fabrics in pink, blue, purple, and green, matching the print in her curtains. I designed a quilt with two dozen game boards, in various shapes and sizes, sparkling against a calm navy background. A rubber ball bounces merrily off the edge. It's a combination of geometry and chaos, a little overboard in places, but quite lovely. Catherine declared, "It's nice, but it's really not my colors." (Well, that was kind of the point.)

Catherine has graduated from college now, a fine young woman with an artist's eye for color and design. She has a strong sense of individual style and prowls flea markets for treasures. I stopped trying to influence her choices long ago and she grew out of wearing underpants on her head, as I knew in my heart she would. At twenty-two, she loves both her baby clothes and her quilts.

Catherine spent the fall semester of her senior year in Uppsala, Sweden, and I visited her there. We spent many hours walking through the town and surrounding countryside. For her graduation present, I decided to give her a down comforter with a pieced duvet cover. For months, I gathered fabrics which reminded me of the earth tones of the houses in Uppsala, the golden autumn leaves, and the light slanting through the trees. I embroidered dozens of stylized flowers. I struggled mightily with patterns, taking the top apart and cutting the pieces smaller. I brought home more fabrics, more patterns. I took pictures at quilt shows. I tried more contrast and less contrast. I sewed and ripped and agonized.

I have a time of uncertainty with every quilt, where my vision and reality collide, the point at which I think, "When there are more blocks . . . if more of it were sewn together . . . once the border is on . . . I will like it more." Then, by the time it's basted, I love it. But with this quilt, the further I got, the more my heart sank. Something was not right—the quilt did not work. Graduation came and I had a box of discards, a wastebasket full of scraps, and a design wall full of blocks, many of them unfinished.

Catherine was tactful and kind. She pointed out the squares she loved. She was enthusiastic about the flowers. She appreciated all the work I'd done, she was touched I would make her a quilt. Alas, gratitude and grace could not make this a better quilt. Neither one of us loved it.

We moved a few blocks around. We selected some fabrics and changed some others. I sewed the blocks together. Finally, she bravely told me she didn't like the border fabrics I had bought.

I knew she was right, but I also knew I had already considered every fabric in our local store. I clung to the faint hope of finding something new—until I saw the shelves emptied for an out-of-town show. But my determined little girl, with her artist's eye and her thrift-store flair, found a half yard of overlooked fabric already cut, tied with twine, and tucked into a corner. It was not an obvious choice: a new color, a different style, an entirely different direction for a quilt which sorely needed to be contained. It was the only piece of that fabric left. It turned out to be perfect, the fabric that made it her quilt. Finally, a happy ending!

Catherine thinks this story is about my struggle to please her. I think it is about my learning to respect her style. We're still talking about it. Together, we will eventually figure it out.

LYNN HEATH *believes it is prudent to keep a well-stocked studio, prepared equally for inspiration and for emergency. Both will come, in due time. "Surround yourself with beauty" may be the best advice she ever read. She has succeeded at this, on many levels, in Charlottesville, Virginia.*

MOMMA'S YO-YOS

- - - - -

RENIE MORSE

My husband and I both volunteer as historical inter-
preters at Lincoln's New Salem State Historic Site, a
preserved nineteenth-century village in Petersburg,
Illinois. Abraham Lincoln lived here for six years when he was a
young adult and it's the place where he started studying the law.
We dress in 1830s costumes and demonstrate the skills appropriate for the time. My husband makes shoes and brooms while I
make baskets and quilts.

One July day, I was working in the Samuel Hill home, where
I was demonstrating the technique of making yo-yo quilts. Yo-
yos are considered a novelty type of quilting and their popularity
comes and goes. Yo-yos are small circles of fabric hemmed on
the edging and with a drawstring, pulled tight into small, com-
pact circles. They are sewed to one another with a slip stitch and
many of them together make a quilt that looks light and airy because there is no backing or batting. But when you hold a yo-yo
quilt, it's actually quite heavy.

I had made a few dozen yo-yos by early afternoon when a
couple in their sixties came to "my" house. When they saw what
I was working on, the man sat straight down on the wooden floor
and began to cry. Not knowing whether he had fallen or not, I
raced around the table to assist. Lots of other people rushed up,
and I was just telling a nearby teenager where to go for help
when the man assured us that he was quite all right. In fact, he

felt wonderful. Well, by that time, he had our undivided attention.

He went on to explain that he was one of ten children and that when he was growing up, his mother would bathe the children and then sit them down with needle and thread to make yo-yos. With that, he picked up a needle and thread from my work table and proceeded to prove that he did, indeed, know how to make them.

No one left the house as he started to tell Momma-stories about his childhood in rural Alabama. Momma had them each make ten yo-yos each night and then she would make them into quilts that she sold to buy extras for her children, like shoes. She read to them while they sewed. Some of the stories were Bible stories and some were from magazines given to her by her employer. The man told us that he preferred short stories because he liked to know how they ended before he went to bed. He had forgotten all about the yo-yos he'd made as a child until he walked in and saw me sewing.

The man and his wife were returning to their home in Detroit when they stopped at New Salem. They had just been to Alabama, where they had buried Momma. While his wife went on to see other buildings, the man stayed with me and made yo-yos for the next four hours. He told me that none of Momma's children had any of her quilts because she had sold them all.

I learned that his mother raised all those children by herself, that she made apple butter and the best corn bread he'd ever had. He said her pork roast was never big enough to feed ten hungry children but he had shoes most of the time as a child. He still loves to listen to books read aloud to this day.

Mostly he talked and sewed without even looking at where the needle was going. He thought maybe he should buy some fabric and make a yo-yo quilt of his own. I told him to take the ones he'd made that afternoon but he said I should put them in a quilt to remember him by.

I did—and I still have that quilt and I still remember him.

RENIE MORSE *and her husband, Ray, live in Two Harbors, Minnesota, with their two golden retrievers. Renie has quilted since childhood, does mosaic, and teaches handmade papermaking around the Midwest. Renie and Ray have been volunteers at Lincoln's New Salem State Historic Site since 1985 and, even after retiring farther north, have managed to volunteer in either the spring or fall.*

MONDAY, MONDAY

- - - - -

T. ATKINS

 I had been working with beaded art quilts for a while when I decided it was time to enter a BIG quilt show to see what others thought of them. I set my sights high and chose the Marin (California) Quilt and Needle Show since it's prestigious, located fairly nearby, gets great press, and has a great reputation. Imagine how I felt when I entered two quilts and one of them received an honorable mention.

The next year, with some judges' critiques under my belt, I requested entry blanks, filled them out, sent in my check, and, upon acceptance, put the date on my calendar when the quilts were supposed to be delivered. Meanwhile, I was asked to put some pieces in a show at the Pumpkin Seed Quilt Gallery in San Raphael, which I happily did, arranging to pick them up just before the start of the Marin show. Well, with quilt beading classes to teach and quilts to make and beads to buy, time passed and life was busy and good.

Late one Monday afternoon, my main squeeze called me from work and asked, "Wasn't this the day you were supposed to deliver the quilts to Marin for the exhibit?"

Oh Help! And also Bother! The pieces were due by five o'clock in Marin, which is about three hours away from where I live, and it was already four. And two of the three pieces I had entered in the show were at the gallery, which was closed on Mondays. Oh Yikes, Drat, Bother, etc.!

Never say die, right? So I got on the phone, first to the Marin County people. Working my way through the hierarchy, I finally got to a person in authority who told me that Betty Murray, the lady in charge of checking people in, was staying at a Hilton next to the convention center, and if I could get my pieces to her by eight that night, all would be well.

Whew! One down!

Next call—the gallery. No one home. Oh, it's Monday, dummy, the day they are closed, remember? So I tried e-mail. No response. Back to my sweetie pie at work, who says, "Oh sure, I'll leave work early, come home, and scoop you up and we can drive up to San Raphael and maybe find somebody there."

So I gathered up the one piece I had at home, "Frog," and off we went. Traffic wasn't bad from home to San Francisco, the Golden Gate Bridge was a piece of cake, and we made it to San Raphael in good time. But when we got there, no lights were on. Nobody was home at all. We checked the back door and the side door and then a woman from the Karate Club next door came over to ask what we were doing. After we explained, she let us use her directory and phone to get in touch with the gallery's owner. Jennifer was at home, fortunately, willing to come down, open the store, and let me have my pieces.

With many thanks, we piled back into the car—quilts, entry forms, and all—and headed to the Marin Convention Center, my sweetie driving while I madly stitched the show's ID numbers to the backs of the quilts we had just picked up. We found the Hilton and Betty Murray, who accepted my pieces in the hotel lobby. She had great smiles for "Frog" and lots of thank-yous.

Having successfully completed our mission, we found a Chinese restaurant and I treated us to a lovely dinner. (You've got to keep your driver happy!)

A week passed and word trickled down that I had received a

ribbon or two. Oh Boy! I'm Excited! Of course I wanted to see the show to check out the competition, all that stuff, you know how it is! So my sweetie and I decided to leave home early, stop at a couple of places along the way, and arrive in Marin in plenty of time to see the show, wait for them to take it down, pick up my pieces, and head for home.

So much for plans. Two or three stops became many and they all took longer than we planned. Traffic wasn't bad until we were through San Francisco and onto the Golden Gate Bridge. There we ground to a halt and when things began to move again, it was start and stop. We finally crept into Marin at six, two hours past closing time, so I never saw the show.

When I got to the head of the line for my first pickup, there was a big hoo-hah because I didn't have my papers, the drop-off being somewhat irregular. But once my identity was settled to everyone's satisfaction, the woman checking me in handed me my beaded "Frog," a handful of ribbons, and an envelope. "There's money in that," she said with a big smile. Surprise! A big check for the Featured Artist award. Then she said, "Come with me, since you don't have any paperwork," and we marched down the hall to pick up my quilts. There were more ribbons and another envelope containing another check, this time for Judges' Choice.

I was feeling more than a little lightheaded by that time. As I trotted down the hall, my arms full of quilts, "Frog," ribbons, and money, one of the attendants for the show stopped me. "I was assisting the table when the judges were judging that quilt," she said, pointing to one of them in my arms. "The judges were saying 'She did this with beads,' and 'She did that with the design,' and 'Look at the textures she created.' When they were all done, I walked over to them and said, 'Yes, and she is a he!'"

I grinned, thanked her for the story, and went to find my wife to tell her that all this trouble had been worthwhile. The Chinese restaurant was closed but we did go to a fabulous (and sinfully expensive) Italian restaurant for dinner. You have to keep your driver happy! (And I figured we deserved it.)

By the way, "Frog"'s real title is *Even Frogs Dream* and his name is really Jason. He garnered three ribbons and a healthy check from that show and he isn't even a quilt. He's a stuffed and beaded velvet animal who sits on a satin lily pad, holding a feather in one paw with which he has written on caladium leaves KISS ME, I'M A PRINCE.

THOM ATKINS *lives in Santa Cruz, California.*

PRESIDENT'S WREATH

A Quilting Adventure

– – – – –

ANN SHIBUT

Often things boil down to who you know. This was certainly the case when I had one of my quilts pictured on the dust jacket of a romance novel! It happened this way.

It was midsummer of 1989. A friend who knew that I was a quiltmaker called to ask if she and her mother could come talk to me about a quilt her mother was going to make. My friend's daughter, then an editor for Simon & Schuster in New York City, had asked her grandmother to make a quilt to be used on a book cover. The grandmother had made quilts before, so it was natural that Linda would think to ask her to do this. The author, Jude Deveraux, and the art director had decided that a quilt would be a good choice for the cover of this particular novel. At that time, Ms. Devereaux had eighteen romance paperbacks in print and was established as a popular and successful author in the romance novel genre.

I wondered why they wanted to talk to me. Then I learned that while the grandmother had made many quilts, all of them were pieced, and the publishing officials wanted a traditional appliqué block in a pattern called President's Wreath for the cover. This old pattern regained popularity around the time that Franklin Delano Roosevelt was president and features a circle with an appliquéd flower marking each quadrant. Traditionally, five leaves are appliquéd (two on the inside, three on the outside) to each portion of the circle that's visible between the flowers, and the finished blocks usually run twelve to thirteen inches square.

I discussed the appliqué process with my friend and her mother, offering opinions and advice on several details. Then I sent them away with my good wishes, expecting to hear no more about it.

Several weeks later, my friend telephoned to say that her mother's health was deteriorating so she would be unable to make the quilt in the required time frame. Would I be willing to let her refer me as an alternative quiltmaker to her daughter the editor? I asked a few questions and then agreed to do it.

I soon received a call from New York City. I learned that the art director had not only selected the pattern but also the desired colors for this cover quilt. Because of the photographic requirements, they had some strict specifications to be met. The rings of the pattern could be no larger than six to seven inches in diameter, much smaller than would be usual, and the quilt should measure about 48 × 60 inches. They wanted an unbleached muslin background and, most important of all, the piece had to be ready to be photographed in a month's time! We agreed on a price and I was excited to get to work.

A packet was delivered by FedEx in a day or two. It included two sketches by the art director showing what they had in mind, plus some Pantone chips to indicate their color selections. I sat down with paper and pencil to draft the pattern and plan the quilt. Because they needed such small rings, I had to eliminate some of the leaves between the four flowers. Three leaves between each blossom seemed right. Since the flowers themselves were so small, I simplified the design even more by using only the basic flower shape plus a center rather than several layers in different fabrics as is usual in such appliqué quilts. I also decided that instead of making individual nine-inch blocks, I could eliminate seams by placing four rings on twenty-inch muslin squares. This made four rings across and five rings down. Translated into "quilt-speak," this meant I would make four large squares and two "half squares" which would speed up the assembly process.

After drawing templates and calculating fabric requirements, I headed to the quilt shop with the little color chips in hand. I was lucky to find materials that matched them all, even the deep blue-green chip. The art director suggested that I use all solid fabrics but I explained that including some prints would be effective, add interest, and also provide a more traditional look for this type of quilt. I was told to use my own discretion.

I cut the shapes from the fabrics and laid them out to form one circular design. It was immediately apparent that the deep green of the twelve leaves per circle was so intense that it over-whelmed the delicate pinks and yellows in the flowers. So I made another trip to the quilt shop, which fortunately had a print fea-turing the same shade of blue-green but a paler tint. This worked better and after I sent swatches to New York, they telephoned their approval and said I should proceed.

By this time it was the first week of October, and I had to have the top appliquéd, assembled, and quilted by the end of the month! I began a whirlwind of stitching. The muslin squares and little pink, green, and yellow pieces went with me everywhere, and I appliquéd every minute I could spare. After assembling the twenty-inch squares, the piece looked unfinished because it had no border. So I added a wide pink one which I knew would not show on the book jacket, but would complete the design nicely for whatever later use it might have.

When my husband and I went to the mountains for his annual fall fishing trip on October 23, I brought along a quilting frame made of lightweight PVC pipe, easily assembled and disassembled.

While John fished, I quilted continually for two days and nights! It was a good thing that only the center of the quilt would show in the photograph, because that meant I did not have to quilt the border or bind it at that point. Still, I had enough time to begin quilting the border when I received a telephone call from the publishers on October 26 saying that they needed the quilt for photography on the following Monday, October 30. I wrapped it and FedEx-ed it to New York the next day.

As soon as they received the quilt, the editor called to say how beautiful she thought it was. She also revealed that in the course of the month while I was sewing, office politics had reared their ugly head. The art director who had planned this cover had been replaced, and the new art director wanted to make "this cover her own," and was suggesting all kinds of changes—including not using the quilt on the cover. I was sorry to hear this but I had already been well paid for my efforts. So there was nothing to do but be philosophical about the situation and wait to see what would happen.

Months went by with no word from New York. Then, in May 1990, I had another telephone call from the editor. She said the book was finally ready, and while they had not used the quilt on the front of the jacket, they had put it on the back, using it as a frame for a picture of the author. She would send me two copies.

When the books arrived, I was so excited! I was surprised to see that they were hardcover books, not paperback as I had thought, a first for the author. The quilt showed up beautifully, and inside the back jacket flap, they credited me as the quilt-maker. I also received a letter from the president of Simon & Schuster in appreciation for the lovely quilt.

After that, whenever I visited bookstores, I always looked to see if the book was available. My sister told me she did the same thing, and that when she saw it displayed, she would turn the copies over so the quilt would show instead of the front cover!

Even though it was featured on a book jacket, the quilt was still unfinished. The editor told me that when she came to Richmond, Virginia again, she would bring it so I could complete the quilting and bind the edges. Again months passed but eventually she came, and for a few days I had the quilt again to do the finishing work, to look at it and compare it with its pretty picture, and to remember the busy days when I was in the midst of this quilting adventure. And after it was finished, what became of my President's Wreath quilt? It was given to the author, Jude Deveraux.

ANN SHIBUT *has been quilting for forty-nine years. She is the editor of* Threads of Thought, *the newsletter of the Richmond Quilter's Guild, and a founding member and past officer of the Virginia Consortium of Quilters. Now widowed, she is retired and enjoys her two sons and daughters-in-law and three granddaughters.*

SOMEONE ELSE'S SCRAPS

- - - - -

BARBARA VALLONE

In the fall of 2004, two of my quilting friends, Mary and Pat, and I decided to hold a charity quilt workshop because we had received lots of fabric scraps and yardage. Mary and Pat did most of the sorting, cutting, and assembling of the "kits" we'd use for our event.

While they were busy sorting and assembling, they got the sneaky idea of putting small scraps, block pieces, ugly fabrics, and other unusable hunks of cloth into theme-related brown paper lunch bags. A few instructions and deadlines were included with these sundries before the tops of the bags were rolled up. Then, one by one, these paper parcels made their way to me as part of a new game that Mary and Pat invented called "Barb's Brown Bag Challenge."

Would you like to see what I received during the first six months of this challenge?

Bag #1—Halloween-related fabrics in squares and strips.
Bag #2—Blocks, block pieces, border strips, pieced borders, and other "stuff."
Bag #3—Solid color fabrics in every shade from pastel to dark.
Bag #4—Authentic 1930s fabric scraps, every one of them an odd shape.
Bag #5—Christmas prints in tans, reds, and greens.

Bag #6—The brightest "you gotta wear shades to look at
them" fabrics you can imagine.

When I received the first Brown Bag Challenge, the Halloween assemblage, I wasn't quite sure what I was going to do
with it. But as I looked through the truly unique fabrics in that
bag, I decided to add two rules of my own to this contest.

1. I am allowed to add yardage in one fabric of my choice.
2. I cannot change the basic shape of the scraps. If they're
    odd triangles, they stay odd triangles. If they have a
    curved edge, they stay curved.

By accepting this challenge from my two good comrades-in-
quilting (and with friends like these, I don't need to search for
any enemies), I have discovered three new, heretofore unknown
rules of quilting that, as far as I know, apply only to Brown Bag
Challenges.

1. No matter how strange the contents of the Brown Bag,
    you will always find the correct, single fabric to add to
    the conglomeration and it will always be on sale.
2. Each bag of fabric will always have "just enough" to
    complete its "chosen" design or layout.
3. You can only decide on a design or layout after all the
    received scraps have been sorted into color families.

I have to say, my Brown Bag Challenge has been a wonderful experience so far. I've made ten lap quilts or wall hangings from the
first four bags. I got a big lap quilt from Bag #1 (that Halloween stuff
just seemed to go a long way), two quilts from the blocks and block
pieces of Bag #2, three quilts from the wide variety of solids in Bag
#3, and four quilts from all that delightful 1930s fabric. I'm not
sure what Bags #5 and #6 hold in store but I can't wait to find out.

Oh yes, that charity quilt workshop that started all of this in the first place was a rousing success. By the end of that Saturday, we had 126 quilts in all stages of development, from pieced tops to finished quilts. Mary, Pat, and I are still working—with the help of lots of other quilters—on finishing all of these projects. As they are finished, they are donated to area nursing homes as well as to the pediatrics and neonatal wards at our local hospital.

Where will my Brown Bag Challenge quilts go? I won't know the answer to that question until they are all finished. But the discoveries I've made about different ways to make useful and colorful quilts from someone else's scraps have been well worth the effort.

BARBARA VALLONE *has been quilting since 1981. She retired from her real-life job in January 2002 to spend more time sharing her love of quilting through teaching basic quilting and other fun classes in and around Racine, Wisconsin. She organizes eight or nine quilt camps a year, coordinates the Quilters Land Cruise each year on the first weekend in March, and lectures to area quilt guilds. You can contact her at QltingB@aol.com.*

BUTTERFLIES

- - - - -

DEE STARK

"I do not know whether I was then a [wo]man dreaming I was a butterfly, or whether I am now a butterfly dreaming I am a [wo]man."

—*Transformations,* Chuang Tzu

In the end was the beginning. In that desolate month of November, when all the world is withering and fading to shades of gray, my grandfather died. The last of that generation in my family, he and I had grown close in the last five years of his long life, talking of things he would never speak of before, sharing laughter and meals and the care of his longtime girlfriend, Marie.

It was no surprise, his passing into a place where he no longer needed his physical body. He had been diagnosed with prostate cancer in his late eighties and chose not to undergo any treatment for it, figuring that whatever time he had left would be more enjoyable without radiation, chemotherapy, or surgery. In his ninety-second year, it spread to his bones but still did not really affect his quality of life and we had two more joyous years. Knowing that someday I would be without him, I treasured the time we had. People say that so often it's a cliché, but I found that, as with many clichés, it was true. And so when he was finally gone, I wanted a tangible way to remember him.

At about the same time, I had my second experience with what I came to regard as my own plastic cocoon. A spinal cord injury and subsequent surgeries left me encased in a rigid body cast for months at a time.

The first time, I thought it was more like a turtle shell for I certainly resembled some poor, overturned amphibian any time I tried to gain my feet. But as much as part of me wanted to pull my head in and withdraw, something deep within me realized I was being transformed. My only choice was what direction that change would take.

So as I lay encased in my cocoon, I sought the reliable comfort of books. I highly recommend learning something new as a distraction when you are trying not to think about what is lost. It's an effective tonic that immediately begins to fill that emptiness with something new and it can help keep life's direction moving forward.

During this time, I was reading everything I could find about the late Victorian period (1875–1901). I felt a kinship with the women of that era, with their confusion and frustration at trying to find a fulfilling role for themselves in a world that was changing at a dizzying pace. I loved to dream of being one of the nouveau riche, of having a large Queen Anne mansion full of Rococo revival furniture, oriental rugs, and objets d'art brought back from my world travels and servants who would care for it all and leave me free to pursue my other interests: playing the piano and needlework.

As I read more and more, I felt like I had been born a century too late, that all that I loved and wanted was suited to a way of life that was long since extinct. During this time of voracious reading, I became intrigued by the Victorian fad of crazy quilting, and the pictures I saw of it had a tremendous appeal. To me, crazy quilting married the best of memorabilia with needlework, and lent itself to self-expression better than any other technique I'd found.

So when Grandpa VanHousen passed away, I claimed his old ties. Not that I was in danger of starting a family feud over them! My grandfather was a kind, gentle man with a pretty hideous fashion sense. Most of the ties were polyester and, of course, his best one was used for the funeral. I took those treasured ties home and put them away. Every time I thought I was ready to use them in a project and took them out, I'd cry and have to put them away again. This went on for six months until I could handle them without being overwhelmed. Finally, I began to stitch a memorial to Grandpa.

At the risk of invoking more clichés, time really did heal. In addition to the ties, I also had unfinished quilt blocks, yards and yards of crocheted pillowcase edging, and a few buttons from my grandmother's sewing box. At first I didn't know what this project was going to be or even what I wanted on it. I did know that I wanted to have a visual and tactile record that would help me remember my grandfather and what he meant to me. As I worked on the blocks, I would take them for my weekly visits with Marie. We grieved his loss, and as we looked at the work-in-progress, we found ourselves crying less and laughing more.

I looked for symbols and motifs that would represent different aspects of what I was trying to say about my grandfather and our family. I discovered that one of my favorite artistic subjects—the butterfly—had a wealth of folklore and meaning attached to it.

I discovered that the lovely lepidoptera has a fleeting time on this earth—an average adult lives but a few weeks. The Greeks gave this species its name and believed that butterflies were an earthly embodiment of the goddess Psyche, who personified the human soul. In Japan, butterflies are believed to be tiny fairies, the holders of fragile beauty, and lovers of flowers (of course!). But my favorite bit of folklore associated with these tiny creatures is the Celtic tradition that butterflies are actually witches that have taken on that shape in order to steal dairy products like butter and milk. It's generally accepted that this is where the English word "butterfly" came from. As a symbol on my grandfather's quilt, it could also represent the belief in the Resurrection that is a core belief in the Christian tradition. That little creature carries quite a load of varied legends on its delicate wings!

As I emerged from my cocoon of isolation and loss, I discovered that I had grown and changed in many ways. I had found soul-satisfying work by creating fiber art, and I'm able to share this love with others through teaching. I continue to feed my intellectual curiosity by researching folklore associated with this uniquely American art form. Crazy quilting arose as a Victorian-era fad and has since survived world wars, the Great Depression, and a clear September day when we and all the world shuddered in horror. What appealed to women in that era of change and chaos in the past continues to appeal to artists today.

In the talk-show pop psychology parlance so popular in our culture, I have "reinvented" myself. This word is ubiquitous today and it can leave us thinking we are so very clever, and we forget the bigger view history offers us. The tiny butterfly has symbolized various cultural concepts since humans have been recording their ideas. I've noticed that without conscious effort, the butterfly has become a recurring thematic image in my fiber art. Sometimes it means one thing to me, the next day it might show a different facet of meaning, but always I remember that quote from the world's most popular author, Anonymous: "If nothing ever changed, there'd be no butterflies."

DEE STARK *has been stitching for more than twenty-five years and teaching for almost ten. Known internationally as an expert on the rich symbolism used in crazy quilting, her research is ongoing. Dee offers lectures and workshops around the world as well as at a local quilt shop. For more information, you can visit her Web site, www.deestark.com.*

ORANGE CURSE

- - - - -

SUSAN BRAZEAL

Most everyone has a color that they don't like or even hate. For me, that color is orange. For years, I quilted orange-free. Then one Saturday, my charity quilting group was chatting about some of the children's quilts we were working on and I declared that I hated orange. Ten minutes later, Rose walks in, a woman who was meeting me to donate three quilt tops for either Project Linus and/or our charity group. The tops were gorgeous but, you guessed it, two of them featured the color orange.

The group admired Rose's tops and told her how wonderful they were. I was assuring Rose that I'd be happy to finish the tops into quilts for deserving recipients when one of my quilting buddies interjected. "But Susan, you hate orange."

Somehow, I resisted crawling under the table and just stood silently, wishing I were invisible.

Fast-forward a couple of years and, while on vacation, I checked the clearance fabric at Hobby Lobby looking for bargains for charity quilts for children. A score—two bolts of NASCAR fabric for $1 a yard! Of course, one of the bolts was of Tony Stewart's number 20 car, the bright orange Home Depot–mobile, but, at that price, I scooped up all six yards. Of course, since I had no fabric to go with it—because I don't like orange—my friends and I had to shop some more.

Now many, many months later, I've finally finished the

twelfth and final orange NASCAR quilt. Or at least I think it's the last one. Twice I thought the last orange NASCAR quilt was done only to find another one of those tops. Recently, there has been a rash of baby quilts to make and, of course, orange has been the best match to the focus fabrics.

So the moral of my story is this: Never declare to your quilting friends that you hate any color, because you will be doomed to use it in quilts forever after.

SUSAN BRAZEAL *enjoys the needle arts, especially quilting and crocheting. She creates her own designs for gifts or easy, quick-to-make items that she donates to charity. Susan shares her designs on her Web site, home.att.net / ~susanbinkc / .*

GEORGIA'S BOUNTIES

- - - - -

MADELINE K. HAWLEY

When I received that first mailing from the Georgia Quilt Project, I just thought, "They've got to be dreaming. Make a quilt for every athlete who participates in the Olympics?" I didn't consider it for five seconds. After all, I have a nine-to-five job as well as being the principal caregiver for a husband who is legally blind and a stroke victim. I'm lucky if I have time to make a quilt for me, I told myself. This project is too ambitious to get off the ground.

But the next thing I knew, the *Atlanta Journal-Constitution* was printing articles praising the Georgia quilters and their incredible and unheard-of idea of making quilts not only for all the athletes, but also for all of the countries participating in the Olympics. The quilt idea seemed to have universal appeal, and the more publicity it received, the more quilters became involved. I started feeling a little twinge of shame for my original lack of enthusiasm.

My friend Shirley Erickson was working on an Olympic quilt and so was my friend Barbara Sanders, but I still dragged my feet. After all, Shirley is a person full of energy, enthusiasm, and ideas who dives into projects and gets wonderful things done. She's also a motivator and can lay quite a guilt trip on you when she has a mind to. As time was running out, Shirley fixed me with a stern look and said, "You really ought to make one, you know." And she had me.

People were already delivering their quilts for the Olympic

Quilt Project when I had just begun to put together some ideas. I needed a focus that could showcase Georgia and simultaneously interest an athlete from another country. Just about that time, I received a copy of the *Market Bulletin* in the mail, a tabloid-type newspaper on Georgia farm produce, plants, and animals. That sparked the idea of presenting the products of Georgia's farms to the athletes of the world.

But what type of produce would best represent Georgia? Peaches, of course, and peanuts and pecans! Consulting the *Market Bulletin,* I found out that cotton is also one of the top farm products of Georgia.

Peaches are easy enough to design and I soon came up with a couple of large, rosy fruits on a stem with leaves attached. The peanuts were a little more of a challenge but I sketched a bag labeled PEANUTS filled with nuts in their shells.

But how in the world should I show a pecan? I think pecan trees are gorgeous, and I love to see a whole orchard filled with them. When I was a child, my whole extended family would go down to the riverbank each fall at harvesting time and spend a day picking up pecans in buckets and bags. We took lunch along and stopped at noon to enjoy a picnic. At the end of the day, we went to the house of the farmer who owned the trees and he divided the nuts we picked up, keeping one half for himself and giving us the rest to take home to enjoy all winter long. I can't tell you the number of winter nights we sat around the kitchen table with Dad cracking the pecans, and the rest of us picking them out of the shells. As I remembered those childhood scenes, I knew how to show pecans—as a tree with its wide, spreading limbs.

With that settled, I just had cotton left to represent. That was easy because I'm a member of the Cotton Patch Quilters and our logo is, what else, a cotton boll. I adapted that and centered it in a quilt block.

I was pleased with the design. With the clock ticking, I tack-led the hand appliqué, starting with the peach block. As I did the handwork, my mind raced ahead to the remaining blocks. I was getting excited about the peanuts. Burlap seemed perfect for the bag, and I decided to stuff the peanuts, making them three-dimensional. The pecan tree could be fused, and then I would finish its edge with a sewing machine blind stitch.

I was racing against time. It took a whole weekend to do the machine quilting but I made the deadline. I had finished *Georgia's Bounty.*

All of the Olympic quilts were to be shown at the Atlanta History Center, and all the quilters received invitations to an evening reception at the opening of the exhibit. There were tables filled with exquisite delicacies to nibble after we strolled through the display of quilts. It was an impressive exhibit, and I was glad Shirley had persuaded me to participate. It created feelings I never would have expected when I first heard about the project.

Prior to the beginning of the Olympics, the Atlanta History Center was open to the public for a special day to see the quilts, buy catalogs of the exhibit, and have all of the quilters available to autograph them. Shirley and I attended, along with my mother and daughter, and we sat with the other quilters autographing the pictures of our work in the catalog. We had not expected to be celebrities! That was a thrill.

The day finally came when a lottery was conducted to de-termine which country would receive which quilt. My quilt was selected go to Swaziland, in Africa, to hang in their Olympic headquarters. I wasn't even sure where Swaziland was, but it didn't take me long to find a map and locate the country, as well as reading as much as I could find out about it.

When I received notification of the time my quilt was to be presented to the athletes and representatives from Swaziland,

I began to plan for the trip to Atlanta. It seemed most efficient to drive to the edge of the city and catch our mass transit, MARTA, for the trip to the Olympic site at Georgia Tech. I'd never ridden a MARTA train before and felt timid about trying it. But then I remembered a former coworker from Emory University and called her to ask if she would like to make a trial run with me. She would. We met in the MARTA station in Decatur a week ahead of the scheduled presentation, rode MARTA, made a transfer to another train, and finally walked to the Olympic site. We made mistakes, had many giggles, and generally had a good time. The trial run made me feel confident that I could find my way on the big day.

On the day Swaziland was scheduled to receive my quilt, I repeated the route I'd scouted and arrived at the appointed time only to discover the presentation had been rescheduled and wouldn't be held until the following day. Of course I was disappointed, having taken a day off from work to make the trip from Athens to Atlanta. But since I was already there, I decided to sit in the area where athletes from other countries were receiving their quilts, and I found it very moving. Suddenly I realized, when Monaco's presentation was announced, that I was sitting across from Prince Albert, Grace Kelly's son! Another unexpected thrill!

As it happened, my bonus day in Atlanta provided the perfect opportunity to explore some of the exhibits and Olympic-related activities without crowds. For example, the High Museum of Art featured The Rings exhibit, and I could stand and absorb each piece of art, taking as much time as I wanted. I can still close my eyes and see some of those works and experience the same feelings of awe I had then. My favorites were the Van Goghs.

Now that I was an experienced Atlanta visitor, I repeated my now familiar routine the next day. This time the presentation took place, as scheduled. Afterward, in the large green tent where receptions were held after each presentation, I met the athletes and dignitaries from Swaziland. They were delightful. A man who seemed to be their leader gave me a flag from their country, an Olympic flag, and a little Swaziland pin from his own lapel. One of the women athletes exclaimed, "Oh, I was hoping we would get that quilt! It was the best one." What a diplomat she'll make someday!

Being involved with the Olympic Quilt Project was one of the more significant experiences in my life, and it changed me in the sense that I am much more receptive to new ideas and to challenges. Who would ever imagine that making one little quilt would bring you into contact with international athletes, allow you to sit across an aisle from a prince, and make you into a book-autographing celebrity for a day?

MADELINE K. HAWLEY, *an Illinois native who now resides in Georgia, spent the majority of her career at the University of Georgia in the area of small business and women entrepreneurs. She is a quilt judge, certified by the National Quilting Association, Inc., and a member of two guilds—Decatur Quilters in Illinois and Cotton Patch Quilters in Athens, Georgia. From a base of traditional quilts, her focus expanded to art and challenge quilts such as the two accepted in the I Remember Mama project, an exhibit shown at the International Quilt Festival in Houston and then as a traveling exhibit in two other locations.*

BACHELOR ON THE PROWL

– – – – –

BELLE McDOUGALL

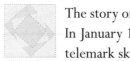 The story of how I met my husband is an unusual one. In January 1997, I was the subject of an article about telemark skiing in a local sports newspaper. The story described a bit about me and my passion for powder skiing. Soon after the article and a photo of me appeared, I received a charming letter from a bachelor who lived not too far away. He kindly introduced himself and added that he hoped we'd get the chance to meet someday.

After I received that first letter, I told my sister about it and asked her if I should write back.

"In this day and age you just never know," she said. However, after reading the letter she thought that I should respond based on two important details—the man's handwriting was incredibly neat and his card was classy.

Soon I got a call from my very concerned mother who had heard about this "bachelor on the prowl." She said, "You're not actually going to write back to him, are you, Belle? I mean, he could be an ax murderer or something!"

I assured her that I would be careful as I popped letter number two in the mail. As the months went by and my relationship with this bachelor progressed to an engagement, my future mother-in-law, Willa, heard about my mother's initial response to her son's charming letter.

"An ax murderer!" she proclaimed with a chuckle as she repeated the story to her family and friends. "Can you imagine?"

Several months before Duncan and I were to be married, my sister-in-law Delia sent postcards to our family and friends asking for volunteers to make squares for a group wedding quilt. She followed up with a package of materials and a deadline date.

Now Willa is very crafty with a needle and thread so she immediately volunteered to join the "wedding quilters' guild." Over the next few weeks, she designed and produced a beautiful and intricately stitched square featuring, you guessed it, an ax.

Apparently when the head quilters received my mother-in-law's square, they didn't quite know what to do with it because its design was not exactly consistent with the overall theme of the project. I'm sure my mother was the one who felt most conflicted about this because she was embarrassed about the "ax murderer" comment she had made. After much discussion and an equal amount of angst, the head quilters made a creative compromise. They left the square out of the quilt but I'm glad to say my husband and I are the proud owners of a pot holder with the most charming ax-murderer motif you've ever seen.

BELLE MCDOUGALL *lives in Waterbury Center, Vermont, with her husband, Duncan, and their son, Jesse. She is a physician's assistant and enjoys piecing together a life with family, friends, hobbies, and sports.*

THREADS

– – – – –

MARY JEWETT

 Her sewing machine was the old-fashioned treadle variety, well used and carefully tended. Colorful calicos and ginghams, cut into tiny squares and triangles, littered her worktable, ready to be stitched into blocks. Spools of thread lined the windowsill. Grandmother made lots of quilts—Bowties, Spinning Bobbins, and sometimes the more difficult Double Wedding Ring.

As a child I would stand beside my grandmother, arranging and rearranging the pieces, discussing the color combinations and patterns. I would hand her each piece as she worked, her foot pumping the treadle. As the blocks emerged from the sewing machine I would trim the threads, press them flat, and stack them neatly on the table. Our heads bent close, our voices low, we discussed many things as we worked—my day at school, small-town news, my dreams for the future. Often she would tell me stories of her childhood—growing up on the farm, her one-room schoolhouse, the county fair where she won her first quilting contest.

For days we worked side by side, building the latest quilt piece by piece. I loved to study each block as it emerged from her machine, looking for the scraps of fabric from garments that once belonged to me. There would always be a fragment of one of my dresses, long outgrown. Today, seeing these tiny reminders worked in with hundreds of other fabrics has the power to evoke long-forgotten memories. The red and white of a bandanna worn at summer camp brings to mind hot summer days spent with friends. The bright blue from my shepherd costume reminds me of the wonder of my first holiday pageant.

When a quilt was finally finished, Grandmother would always stitch the date onto a corner of the blanket. While she claimed she could no longer see to thread the needle or that her arthritis was acting up, her embroidery was beautiful. I suspect she made these claims to give me this task knowing the pride I would feel when I handed her the threaded needle. I would then slip the embroidery hoops into place and watch as she pulled the thread in and out, the thimble sparkling on her finger. Those simple letters and numbers feel like braille against the soft fabric.

Then, with a flip of her wrists, she'd snap the quilt into the air and I'd watch it float for a moment before settling across the table, where I smoothed it flat with the palms of my hands. This would be our first look at the completed project—our first look at the repeating pattern of the fabrics and colors creating the blocks.

All the major events and milestones in my life were marked with the gift of a quilt from my grandmother. On the first day of kindergarten, I received the Schoolhouse pattern—the schoolhouses worked in bright red calico against a brilliant white background. On my sweet sixteen, she surprised me with the Flower Basket pattern in blues and yellows. And for my wedding, a lovely Double Wedding Ring in a variety of pastels. She had kept these projects hidden from me, working only when I was not around. She took pleasure in my surprised delight.

The patterns of the blankets mirrored the patterns of my life. Each new quilt was a new set of stories. All the things we had discussed over the hum of the sewing machine, all her memories from the past and my dreams for the future were as connected to the quilt as if they were written on the blocks.

I have always loved these quilts and used them with carefree abandon in my younger days, always believing there would be more, as we often do when we are children. Some of my blankets are now so worn, the batting pokes through the shredded fabric. But I will not part with them. Instead I fold them carefully, wrap them in tissue paper, and store them in my cedar chest, where they will be safe from further wear and tear. I never told my grandmother I did this. She would not have been pleased.

"A quilt is made to be used," she would say. Above all else, she was practical.

I believe a quilt must be created by a loved one for a loved one. Each square is cut by hand, the pattern carefully planned, the fabrics chosen by a person whose own memories are represented by the pieces.

I often wonder what my grandmother thought about while stitching a tiny square of my first school dress to a piece of her old apron, the thread binding the pieces securely. No scrap of fabric was ever wasted. While the quilt itself might be a sentimental reminder of important events, holding on to the dress or apron would have been a waste of material.

Grandmother is gone now. While I miss her no less as the years pass, when I remove one of her quilts from my cedar chest and shake out the folds, she is still with me. I feel her steady hand on my shoulder, reminding me of my history and who we are, watching me as I go about my life.

I can retrace her life and mine by spreading a quilt over my bed. Draping one around my shoulders feels the same as her arms around me, safe and warm. I hear the echo of her voice in my ears as I remember the things we spoke of. Her stories always had a cleverly disguised lesson hidden within, although I did not see this at the time. I simply enjoyed the tales.

She gave me a gift by entrusting me with the stories of her life. It is a gift I am sharing with the next generation of my family—retelling her tales of joy and hardship, love and laughter. By listening to my dreams, she gave herself the ability to glimpse my future—a future she would not be a part of. At least not in the physical sense.

But she will always be with me. Our lives are as interwoven as the blankets we created. We are bound together by similar threads.

MARY JEWETT *lives in DeSoto, Kansas, with her soulmate, Mark. She writes with retrievers Grace and Lucie Belle at her feet, snoozing on a Bowtie quilt made by her grandmother.*

SPECIAL NEEDS

- - - - -

SYLVIA LONGWORTH

At some point in their quilting lives, I'm sure every quilter pieces together a gift for someone they love. I'm convinced that when we do this, our quilts become so saturated with our emotions, they end up doing more than keeping someone warm. They keep someone loved.

I belong to a group called Tender Loving Quilters. It was formed in 1994 in a small town in Massachusetts. There are currently twenty-one loving and giving women in the group who come from various walks of life, but who share a common thread, "the love of quilting."

We meet once a week and our focus is making quilts to donate to newborns who require special-needs care in our local hospital. In addition, we donate quilts to seriously ill adults and children to comfort them during their illnesses. To date, our group has made and donated more than a thousand quilts.

Nowadays, more and more babies are being born who require special-needs care so the demand for our quilts is too often greater than we can supply. When the medical staff at our local hospital receive our quilts, they are spread on top of the incubators the babies are using. Then when they get to go home, the quilts are sent along with them. The medical staff have told us many times that we must put a lot of love into our quilts because the recovery rate of the babies who receive them seems to be quicker and more successful.

I am sure they are right, because I've seen it happen firsthand when a baby in my extended family developed very serious medical problems following his birth. These problems required him to be transferred to an out-of-state, special-needs baby care hospital. One of our quilts went along with him. That child's parents believe the love in that quilt must have been extra special, because in a little over a week, their baby was able to return home. He has since celebrated his first birthday and is healthy and beautiful.

But while this child came home, his quilt didn't. When the parents and the boy were about to leave, the medical staff at that hospital asked if they could have the "quilt" for another very ill baby in their nursery who needed tender loving care. The answer, of course, was yes. Love, after all, is meant to be shared.

SYLVIA LONGWORTH *married early in life and has a daughter and a son. She worked for the famous golf-ball maker Titleist for thirty-two years. She's retired now and just celebrated her fiftieth wedding anniversary. She loves to travel with her husband in their motor home. She now has five precious grandchildren and two great-grandchildren.*

PROJECT LINUS

- - - - -

JOAN FINLEY

I started working with Project Linus the year after it started—1996, I think it was. I have a nephew who's handicapped, and at the time, my sister-in-law was ill with cancer and I felt helpless. Then I read about Project Linus in a magazine and I thought, That's something I can do. Project Linus is a national program that takes donations of handmade quilts or afghans and distributes them to critically ill or traumatized children. I am the local coordinator for my area.

It's funny, the blankets seem to arrive in spurts. Up here in Vermont where it's so cold in the winter, you'd think that people would be doing warm projects like quilts or afghans but some winter months go by with no blankets. Then the next month, I'll have over a hundred blankets come in at once.

Except in an emergency like 9/11 or Hurricane Katrina, all of the blankets that I receive are distributed to children in our local hospitals, through a visiting nurse association that visits needy families with newborns, and a nonprofit that provides a haven for children who are undergoing outpatient treatment at our medical center. I log each afghan, blanket, or quilt that I receive and to this date, I've distributed 3,200 of them.

When I go to do a distribution, I have a friend who always comes with me and we've seen some pretty touching things. One of the most memorable involved a visit to our medical center, which has a section specifically set aside for children, the Children's

Hospital at Dartmouth (CHaD). When you first walk in, you see the infants and as you go farther into CHaD, the ages of the patients rise. One day, my friend and I were delivering blankets there to a list of patients given to us by the head nurse. The last name on this particular list was Charlie, a seventeen-year-old boy.

"I don't know if you're going to want to go into his room or not," the nurse said.

"Why not?"

"He's just miserable because he thinks that at seventeen, he should be in the adults' ward and he's really unhappy about being in here," she said. "Nothing we've tried seems to help."

My friend and I looked at each other. "Well, we'll see how it goes when we get there," I said.

So we started making our rounds, taking two or three blankets at a time into each room so that the patients or their parents, if they were in the room, could have a choice. When we got to Charlie's room, his mother was sitting outside his door, reading a book. We told her why we'd come and she said the same thing as the nurse.

"I don't know how he'll react," she said. "He feels it's bad enough that he's in the hospital but it makes it much worse for him being in the children's section. It's been so hard to help him, because he's so unhappy."

"Well, can we try?" I asked.

She raised her eyebrows doubtfully but said yes. At that point, we had two quilts that were the right size for a boy his age. I can't remember what kind of fabric was in one of them but I do remember that the second quilt had dogs on it. My friend and I picked them up and walked in, explaining to Charlie that we were from Project Linus, and told him a little bit about it.

He took one look at the dog quilt and reached out his hands. Tears started to roll down his face as he pulled it to him. When he could finally get a word out, he said, "It looks like my dog and it's been so long since I've seen him." And then he cried even harder. Startled, his mother came in. After a few words of explanation, my friend and I quietly stepped out of Charlie's room, both of us struggling with our own tears.

As we left, the head nurse approached us, asking about Charlie.

"He cried," I said.

She looked stunned. "Charlie cried?"

At those words, every other nursing ear turned toward us. "Charlie cried?"

We nodded again and suddenly, nurses were hustling down the hall, all eager to witness the small miracle wrought by a quilt with dogs on it. I don't know if that change in his personality lasted for an hour or a day or for the rest of his stay, but I do know that the gift of that quilt reached him.

That's what makes it all worthwhile.

JOAN FINLEY *lives in Hartland, Vermont, where she was born and brought up. She is married, has two children, and two grandchildren. She learned to sew at a very young age and continues to enjoy all aspects of the craft, in particular making quilts for family and friends. In 2006, she passed her volunteer activities with Project Linus on to another coordinator.*

A GIFT OF LOVE

- - - - -

CAROL B. FUCHS

It was an amazing sight: six teenagers, lots of well-worn sheets piled high on a table, an equal pile of lightweight cotton blankets with designs of every description—from floral to plaid, stripes, nursery rhymes, cowboy scenes, and bold prints in bright colors—and two old black sewing machines, scissors, red and blue pencils, an iron, an ironing board, and a few rulers. We were ready to begin. All we needed was the volunteer who had offered to help us learn how to put together a quilt. And, as we were about to find out, we would need lots of patience.

None of us had ever worked on anything quite like this before but all of us were excited to get started. We were going to make "a blanket for Bangladesh"! And although these teens didn't have any idea where Bangladesh was (until we went to the library and located it on a map), they could all identify with the orphans who lived there without much clothing and few blankets to keep them warm at night.

"Wow," said one of the boys when he heard why we had been asked to do this. "I used to share a blanket with my little brother. But at least we had a blanket to share."

They all knew how welcome their quilt would be and worked on it throughout the week as though it was a very special gift of love. Which is exactly what it was.

These young people were participants in an academic enrichment program at Dartmouth College. They came to the college
from under-resourced urban and rural communities for two
weeks every summer during high school. In addition to the academic curriculum which we had designed for them, they were
introduced to a variety of new and unusual activities. Sewing, by
their own admission, would indeed be "new and unusual." And
learning how to use a sewing machine would, most certainly, give
them something to talk about when they returned home.

Four of the six students were African-American, one was
Native American, and one was Hispanic. They didn't look alike
but they had everything else in common: they came from single-
parent families, lived in poverty-level neighborhoods, and had
academic potential but hadn't yet been "turned on" in school.
Their goal was to graduate from high school and go to college, although they weren't too sure how that would happen, and their
parent or guardian supported that dream.

When they arrived at Dartmouth, these six teens were each
matched with a mentor from the college. These mentors were
Dartmouth students spending the summer between their sopho-
more and junior years on campus. The mentors welcomed the high
school students as they arrived from their home communities and
spent parts of the next two weeks helping these ninth graders ad-
just to life in a dormitory, talking about the importance of getting
a good education, of respecting diversity, of listening to each other,
and helping to create a community of concern for the needs of
others as well as their own. (At the end of the two weeks, the college students admitted that they had, quite possibly, received more
from this experience than they could possibly have given.)

So there they were, six big strapping boys eagerly waiting for
their turn at the sewing machines and a chance to try to stitch the

squares which we had measured, cut, and assembled. Using the machines looked easy when the instructor demonstrated the technique but coordinating the pedal with the needle on the material took some practice. These tall basketball players, so coordinated on the court, had a very difficult time with this. The thread broke or became tangled or the pedal refused to move and then surged ahead with no warning. The stitches were uneven or too loose and had to be pulled out and redone.

On the other side of the room, a junior varsity quarterback and a wrestling champion hunched over the frame on which the quilt was stretched. They desperately tried to thread a needle with yarn and then struggled to topstitch the finished squares which our instructor pieced together the night before.

There was lots of nervous laughter. Lots of language that they later apologized to me for having used in my presence. Lots of protests about not being able to do this. And then, realizing what they had done, the room became very quiet.

The lines of topstitching weren't quite straight. The pattern was a bit bizarre. (In some places, the colored squares "fought" with each other for visual attention.) But the quilt was finished. Carefully, they removed it from the frame and wrapped it around themselves. Big smiles reflected their pride while a few tears betrayed their emotions.

Once again, this group had beaten the odds and done something others wouldn't have thought they could accomplish. They had made a blanket to send to Bangladesh. Six high school students from poor neighborhoods, who were lucky enough to have blankets of their own, would be part of an effort to make this world a little warmer for someone in a land they had never heard of until that week. Someone who had even less than they did. There would be lots to talk about when they got home.

CAROL B. FUCHS *lives in Hanover, New Hampshire. She is on the Executive Committee of the Summer Enrichment at Dartmouth (SEAD) program for high school students from under-resourced urban and rural communities throughout the United States. This story is an account of her first encounter with quilting, an experience she shared with six teens from SEAD.*

POHAI KE ALOHA

(Circle of Love)

PATRICIA LEI MURRAY

It was morning. Long shafts of sunlight sliced through the misty forest rain. We were all at Brother Laka's home in Volcano to celebrate Mom's eightieth birthday. My sisters and I had waited for this weekend for a long time. Then tragedy struck. Tippy, my mother's pet poodle and dear companion of many years, accidentally died. All of our happiness turned into a deep, piercing *'eha*. How we ached for our mother as each of us, four grown daughters, formed a *pohai ke aloha*, a circle of love, to bear her up.

The day took on an immediate and purposeful direction as each of us set out to assist in a proper burial for Tippy. Mom decided to accept Laka's offer to bury her dear companion there, on his property, among the *hapu'u* ferns and the *'ohi' a lehua*.

Each of us knew, instinctively, what our assignments were. Without a word, Kanani took a basket and went out to gather flowers and ferns to *wili* a special *lei*. Leo and Rosanne planned a burial service and chose music. It was decided that I would make a quilt for Tippy.

We each offered a piece of our clothing for the *kapa,* or blanket. Rosanne offered her white shawl, Leo her favorite Tahitian T-shirt, Kanani the hem of her shirt (which I braided), Laka a piece of red fleece, Mom the scarf she wore on the daily walks she took with Tippy, and I contributed the sleeves of my flannel nightshirt. It was amazing how the quilt took loving shape, a humble collage of Aloha.

During the service, we reached back into our Hawaiian heritage, singing songs of comfort and offering solace for our mother. The singing was healing. It awakened us to our gifts and our strengths. It unified us.

As we walked over to the place of burial, it rained. All you could hear were the raindrops on our umbrellas and the birds singing high in the *'ohi' a lehua* trees, reminding us that what the Lord giveth, the Lord taketh away, in His own time and in His own way. How compassionate was his love to put us all together on that appointed day so that we could truly "be there" for our mother and for each other, to feel the grace of His comforting hand.

PATRICIA LEI MURRAY *is a native Hawaiian quilter who is currently the president of the Hawaiian Quilt Guild. She has been quilting for about thirty years, specializing in both traditional and contemporary Hawaiian quilts. She is the author of* Hawaiian Quilt Inspirations: A Journey of Life.

THE FAMILY THAT QUILTS TOGETHER...

- - - - -

SUANN COLE

 It all began with Grandma Seedorff, a prolific lifelong quilter who created a Christmas quilt to hang in her home. Of course, all the daughters and granddaughters thought it was wonderful but Grandma wasn't really prepared to make one for each of them. After all, she makes quilts for each of the grandchildren as they graduate from high school as well as many other quilting projects for the daughters and in-laws. Well, if Grandma couldn't make one for each of us, maybe we should make them for ourselves. And thus the Seedorff Quilt Tradition was born.

The first set of rules was simple:

- Anyone in the family who was at least twelve years old could participate.
- Each participant would make a block, Grandma would put them together and then finish the quilt.
- Every Christmas, a name would be drawn to receive it and then the process would start all over again.
- Once someone agreed to be part of the project, they had to stick with it until everyone received their quilt.

As it happened, there were twelve people willing to make blocks, including one grandson, so it was easy for a layout of three-by-four. The first quilt was made with a Christmas theme. It featured simple stars and trees for the nonquilters and Santa faces for the more experienced. When it came time for the drawing, the lucky winner was the only male in the group, the grandson named Robert.

During the showing of that first quilt, some of the grand-daughters wanted to know if the theme always had to be Christmas. They wanted something they could use all the time, especially since some were getting close to graduating and didn't want to wait for a home of their own in order to use it. It sounded like a good idea but this meant a rules change. So we decided to draw the winner's name at the beginning of the cycle in order to give the person a chance to choose the pattern and colors they liked for their quilts.

Like most "new traditions," ours kept evolving. To help keep the choice of pattern simple, one of the daughters-in-law made up samples of blocks that were easy enough for all the participants, then that year's winner chose a block from the samples. In order to make the blocks look more connected, everyone used the same background fabric, and this was distributed with directions that Grandma and the daughter-in-law typed up. And we moved the drawing date up to Thanksgiving.

Once we had the process down, it quickly became apparent that we could make two quilts a year though they're still made in the order in which the winners' names are chosen. We often get complaints about the difficulty of someone's chosen pattern, but I've noticed that when it's your turn, difficulty is not your main concern.

Some of the participants ask the quiltmakers to sign their individual blocks while others want all the signatures on the back. Regardless, each of us has a truly special family memento. Of course, once we've made the twelfth quilt, we have to figure out what comes next!

SUANN COLE *lives in rural Missouri with her husband and son. Quilting has been a longtime passion of hers. Friends and relatives have been happy recipients of many of her quilts.*

CRAZY ABOUT YOU

--- --- --- ---

I'd been editing my guild's newsletter for a number of years when I finally decided I was ready to give up the job. This was, coincidentally, around the same time that my partner of many years, Nate, and I decided to get married. At the board meeting when I announced I was ready for a replacement, one of the other members jokingly asked what I was going to do with all my spare time. "Well, I'm going to be planning a wedding—mine!" I replied.

We found a replacement editor for the newsletter who was willing to take over right away and the timing turned out to be fortunate because in the subsequent months, things became very difficult for our family. My sister-in-law was murdered. A family at the small school that our son attended lost a child at birth. Then we learned that a longtime friend had developed a brain tumor. And just before our guild's annual quilting retreat, the man accused of my sister-in-law's murder hanged himself in prison.

Even though I was not really in the mood, I decided to go ahead and attend the retreat. On the drive there with my friend Ginger, she was stitching a crazy quilt block. I'd heard talk about a crazy quilt that some members of the guild were working on but I just couldn't work up the enthusiasm to take on another project.

There were a number of women working on the crazy quilt blocks at the retreat and I admired them whenever they started setting the blocks out on the floor. The colors were so rich—greens, golds, and reds in luscious fabrics like velveteens and silks along with cottons, all decorated with intricate embroidery and embellishments.

My project was a Tumbling Blocks quilt that I'd started in a workshop. I designed a border for it then finished sewing most of it. One of the guild members encouraged me to enter it in our state's quilt festival and even took a picture of my unfinished project so I could send it in with the application.

I returned from the retreat and threw myself into wedding preparations—and into finishing my quilt for the festival.

At a guild meeting a few weeks later, several members got up to make a presentation. They brought out this absolutely gorgeous queen-sized crazy quilt in rich fabrics with wonderful embellishments. I was overwhelmed when I found out it was a wedding gift for Nate and me. Many of the blocks were personalized with photos, initials, and details specific to our life together such as windmills (we have a windmill for power), trapezes, quilts I'd made, a car Nate built, logos for the school our children attended, and a newspaper published by my parents. I was touched by the generosity, caring, and skill of my friends but I couldn't stop laughing at the downright sneakiness with which they'd worked on the quilt right in front of me, carefully hiding the personalized blocks and showing me only the "anonymous" ones.

That summer, I got the pleasure of seeing two of my quilts at the festival—my Tumbling Blocks quilt and the guild's gift. To make it even better, that incredible wedding present received a special award for the best crazy quilt that year.

NELLIE PENNINGTON *lives with her family and quilts in a solar-and wind-powered home in Vermont. She is a member of the Northern Lights Quilt Guild in Lebanon, New Hampshire.*

HANNAH'S QUILT

- - - -

BECKY ROWBOTTOM

Needles and thread, needles and threads, the natural extensions of my mother's fingers—fingers that were never at rest. Her handiwork helped her get through times of great stress and sorrow: a beloved brother's death in a mining accident during the Depression when she was a young girl, fear for the safety of family members overseas during World War II, the death of a thirteen-year-old daughter who was ill from infancy. While sitting in her easy chair at night, appliquéing a quilt top, she displayed a serenity seen at no other time. This is why her disinterest in all things creative was so heartbreaking to see after the death of my father. Nothing could reawaken her and I believe the loss of this once-pleasurable activity contributed to her mental decline.

She came from her home in western Pennsylvania to live with me in upstate New York for that last year of her life, a broken shell of a woman, lost in a body which had betrayed her, the multiple myeloma slowly taking her life away. During that year, I was working on a baby quilt for my first grandchild. I had designed it in a Storybook pattern with each square depicting one of my daughter's favorite childhood tales. At night, as I sat appliquéing Babar's crown, or the butterfly on Bambi's tail, I would listen to my mother's labored breathing as she puttered around, and prayed she would live long enough to see her great-grandchild.

For the first month after her arrival, Mom showed no interest in my sewing room except to say, "You have too much stuff!" as she wandered through it on her way to her bedroom. But as the weeks passed, I noticed that she slowed down as she passed through to see what had been added to my design wall the previous night. Then she began to go through my fabrics, suggesting this one for Madeleine's hat, that one for Tinkerbell's wings. As winter passed into spring, she became an enthusiastic participant in the Storybook quilt, that creative spark once more shining in her tired old eyes.

Her namesake, Hannah, was born in April in Richmond, Virginia, the news of her arrival coming as Mom was receiving chemotherapy. A month later, twenty-four hours after little Hannah was wrapped in her Storybook quilt and placed in her arms, my mother died.

But the torch has been passed. Six-year-old Hannah loves my sewing room and has picked up her own needle and thread. Someday she will understand the role her "Grandma-Grandma Anna" played in the creation of one of her most beloved possessions.

BECKY ROWBOTTOM *had a needle put in her hand at the age of six and has been quilting and sewing ever since. Raised in Pennsylvania, she moved to Oneida, New York, when her husband began his oral surgery practice in 1976 and began a lifelong love affair with the Adirondack Mountains and the farmlands of central New York. When not quilting, she practices yoga, bakes "Grandma Becky's Special Cookies," and gives thanks for a husband who understands that his shirts aren't clean, because there's a new batch of fat quarters in the washing machine.*

THE QUILT THAT WAITED

- - - - -

SALLY WATSON

I love to quilt, it's as simple as that. My very first quilt was a Weathervane pieced in a lovely green kettle cloth with a yellow paisley print and white broadcloth. For those of you who may not know what a Weathervane pattern looks like, imagine a small square surrounded by a much larger square that's been turned 45 degrees (like a diamond). Now add to that four chunky arrows whose points pierce the larger square to touch the corners of the first. (I'll wait while you draw a diagram.)

Anyway, a great deal of polyester made it into that first quilt, something that's now a no-no but you have to remember that this was 1974, and there was not as much quilting fabric available then as there is now. It took three months to assemble that top of twenty-one pieced blocks, twenty-one alternate blocks, and a simple green and white border bound in yellow. This was the quilt I wanted to have on my bed in college and I did finish it, just not on time.

While I was quilting the Weathervane quilt, I decided to start another top. Some of Mom's friends quilted and they gave me some scrap material. I added some I'd collected from sewing my own clothes as well as other projects, and decided to make Shoofly blocks, hand pieced. Shoofly blocks have a square of one color in the center with triangles of the same color touching each of its corners. The rest of the block is filled in with squares or triangles of a different color. In all, there are thirteen individual pieces of fabric in a Shoofly.

Well, I kept my Shooflies, ready to piece, in a little cigar box that I used for storage. Sometimes I would quilt on my Weathervane and sometimes I would piece my Shoofly blocks. I made a lot of these blocks off and on over the years. I also made a lot of other quilts—Cheater's cloth quilts, pieced quilts, appliqué, silkscreen when I didn't have the time to appliqué, and whole cloth quilts. I tied quilts, quilted by hand, machine quilted, and did quilting on the go. I tried it all and I even finished the Weathervane. But those Shoofly blocks were still hanging around.

Then in the late 1980s, Gwen Marston gave a talk and workshop at our guild. What a wonderful time we had! She showed a simple dark and light Nine Patch quilt in a red streak of lightning setting. One look at that quilt and I knew what to do.

The next day, I went on a hunt for the right fabric and found the perfect green for a streak of lightning for my Shoofly blocks. In less than a week, that quilt top was finished. It was fifteen years from first stitch to finished top but I still wasn't done. That poor Shoofly project went back into the linen closet because I had no idea how I was going to quilt it.

Meanwhile, it was time to buy a new house. We moved in 1994 and one of my friends offered to let me try her quilting frame for a while. Well, I found an old book that I had read cover to cover countless times in high school, and in rereading it, I saw a mention of a quilting pattern called Baptist or Methodist Fans. At last I knew how my Shoofly should be quilted—and only twenty years after that first block.

I really enjoyed working on that quilt in the new house that first winter. Our son was three and a half and our daughter barely two. They played in the basement so I could keep an eye on their adventures while I worked on the Shoofly. Well, before long they got interested in my quilting. So I showed them how to pull the needle through for me. Then they wanted to stitch. So I gave them each a larger (and less pointy) needle filled with perle cotton. I dragged out some stools so they could reach and started them in the center square of a Shoofly block. They'd hop on the stool, push the needle into the quilt, hop off to run under the quilting frame, pull the needle all the way through, and push it back up again. Now as you can imagine, this method doesn't guarantee the most even stitches. But do you know, they are still in place and my son is now in high school.

Those stitches make the Shoofly quilt extra warm, and because of that, it will always be among my favorites. I'm glad it waited.

SALLY WATSON *lives in Richmond, Virginia, with her husband, Frank, and three children, Stephen, Kelsey, and Richard. A licensed architect, she currently teaches computer technology at St. Bridget's School.*

RESCUE MISSION

- - - - -

CAROLYN LAUING-FINZER

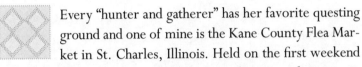 Every "hunter and gatherer" has her favorite questing ground and one of mine is the Kane County Flea Market in St. Charles, Illinois. Held on the first weekend of every month, it's a myriad of dealers who routinely set up in prime locations among the ten pavilions and open-field venues on the twenty-nine-acre fairgrounds. One of the regular attendees is an architectural salvage company from Chicago. It specializes in things such as wrought-iron grillwork, terra-cotta facade blocks, ornamental urns, and lots of bric-a-brac.

While browsing one afternoon, I was aghast to find that the truck drivers for this salvage company had wrapped all of their heavy remnants in quilts that were being used as packing blankets and ground cloths. They'd been dragged through the crushed limestone covering the vehicle lanes and some of them had oil stains.

My rescue mission instincts kicked into high gear. Mike, "the head man of recycled buildings," told me that an African-American woman had made forty of these colorful, randomly patterned, polyester patchworks. She died rather young, leaving no family and no instructions about where her quilts should go. So Mike decided they would make dandy drop cloths and packing for things like cornice carvings, large welded iron gates, and fencing.

I chatted with Mike about these unique pieces of fiber art and expressed the decided opinion that what they needed was TLC and, above all else, appreciation and dignity. To see them lying dirty on the ground just broke my heart!

He asked if I would like to pick one out and take it home with me. Did I? There was one that seemed to be saying "adopt me, adopt me." It was a glorious assemblage of four-inch squares with strip sashing dividing rows of sixteen units per block. One fabric in particular caught my eye, a violet flower motif. My Girl Scout camp name is Violet.

Cleaning the quilt was a challenge. I vacuumed. I tumbled it in a gentle-cycle dryer. I hung it in the fresh air on a clothesline and voted not to wash it lest the stitching unravel.

My rescued quilt's coming-out "Cinderella Party Debut" was the annual Naper Settlement Quilt Show at the nearby historical village. From treasure to trash to treasure, my rescued quilt had come full circle.

CAROLYN LAUING-FINZER *is an energized, eclectic woman who wears many hats: artist, teacher, public speaker, model, professional story-teller, award-winning environmental gardening advocate, and jovial "junk-yard gypsy." She is a member of the Naperville, Illinois, Riverwalk Quilters Guild and has over ninety antique and new quilts in her personal collec-tion, over half of which were found at garage sales, resale shops, and flea markets. She shares many of these quilts with the public at local quilt ex-hibitions, telling their unique stories.*

ARTFULLY FOUND

– – – – –

NANCY VASE

At first, it was just another assignment on a hot, sweaty May afternoon as I waited in a small-town high school art class for a bunch of lively and talented students to gather for me to take their picture for the local newspaper. It was obvious they were far more interested in planning their weekend activities and horsing around than in posing for this "old lady" photographer. But their artwork, which was lined up around the room, was going to the state high school art contest, and its quality testified to their ability if not their attitude.

"Wait here. Take a seat and I'll go get the others," the art teacher said to me as she smiled and dashed out of the room. I picked a seat that didn't have any paint or suspicious spots on it—and waited. As I glanced around the room at some of the other wonderful pieces of artwork that didn't make it to the state level, my gaze passed a stack of wrapped items on a wide shelf along the wall. And snapped back.

One of the flat items was in an unusually colorful wrapping. I looked around for the teacher, just like a guilty student might, then rose and crossed the room to the suspicious pile.

The second item down was wrapped in pink and green and plaid—a quilt! I carefully lifted the top painting on the pile and I could see Nine Patches on point, bordered by a faded but formerly very bright pink with sawtooth edges equally faded but once bright green. The quilt was made of some solids but most of it was plaids. Yes, it was definitely a quilt but now it was covered with spots, gobs and blobs of paint, plaster, rust, dirt, mud, and who knows what.

Just then, the door flew open to admit a herd of moving teenagers followed by the art teacher. They picked up their art pieces and lined up obediently, joking quietly among themselves. "They're all here," the teacher announced, making sure they were all presentable and smiling while she wrote out their names in proper order for the picture's cutline.

After one good photo and two more for insurance, the photo session was all over. The students exploded into normal teenage volume and dashed away. That's when I had my chance.

I approached the teacher and asked my fateful questions: "Where did the quilt come from? Who did it belong to? Would you think of letting me rescue it? Would it even be salvageable?"

The teacher pondered and said, "I don't know but I'll ask," then went into the next room. Before long, the department head entered, introduced himself, and explained that the quilt had been there for quite a few years and he didn't know who had brought it into the school in the first place. They used it to "protect" student art that was being transported, he said.

"Egad," I thought, "that much is disturbingly evident." But as I minded both my manners and my tongue, I asked if they would inquire about ownership, and if no one claimed it, what would they want for it, and would they consider letting me have it? The department head said he would ask around while the art teacher quietly mentioned that the department had a new ceramics kiln but no money to pay for the necessary electrical connections. I gave the teacher my phone number.

It took a few days but my phone finally did ring. It seemed that no one on the faculty or in the administration could remember when or how the orphaned quilt had appeared. But they did agree that it would be acceptable to sell it if the money could benefit the art department. It seemed that it would cost $100 for an electrician to hook up the new kiln. I thought that was a bargain.

It took four soakings in the bathtub but almost all of the stains, plaster drops, and paint came out. The former brightness of the fabrics was now charmingly evident. In fact, my orphaned quilt was in remarkably good condition when it was cleaned up. But as I soaked it, I kept wondering, Who had abandoned this quilt? Did they think it was ugly? Didn't they like the plaid? Did a child simply take it to school and forget it? Was someone missing it?

I finally folded it lovingly and placed it in the closet with my other quilts until I could find just the right spot to display it. The orphan looked so glad to have found a home at last.

A quilter since 1967, NANCY VASE *has had a recent quilt,* Ariadne's Thread No. 1, *published in the* Art Quilt Engagement Calendar 2006. *She continues to design and machine quilt her creations in southwest Wyoming, where she lives with her family and two dogs. She continues to watch for quilts in need of rescue in both the usual and unusual places.*

THE SECRET OF THE PLACERVILLE QUILT

- - - - -

BETTY WILL

 Never in my wildest dreams did I ever think I would find such a surprise at the end of the day at the Placerville (California) Antique Street Fair.

It was my birthday, and my first time out of the house after orthoscopic surgery on my knee in September 2004. Whenever my husband and I go to fairs like this, we're always on the lookout for a certain few items—American art pottery, vintage linens, political campaign buttons, black transferware, and crazy quilts. But to our disappointment, that day we found nothing. At least, not until the end of the afternoon when the vendors started packing up their wares along the main thoroughfare.

Just as we were about to leave, I spotted it, folded among other linens hanging over a rod. At first, it looked like a small child's or doll's quilt, but as I began to unfold it, I discovered it was a large, full-sized brightly colored crazy quilt. Some of the silk pieces in it definitely showed their age, but the rest was in quite good condition, mostly rich damasks, velvets, taffetas, satins, and sateens.

We asked the price and since it was the end of the day, the vendor said we could have it for $75. I thought that was a really good price, as its apparent age told me it was worth much more. But my husband quickly began to point out, "It's very worn here and it would take a lot of work to repair it. Look here, some of these patches are falling apart," he said, pointing to a few of the silk pieces. He was in his full-blown negotiation mode. I knew the disintegration of the silk was clear evidence of the age of the quilt. But the vendor, hurrying to pack up and leave, agreed with my husband.

"Yes, some pieces are pretty worn," she said. "You can have it for fifty dollars."

Hoping to gain some information about the quilt's provenance, I asked, "Do you know who made the quilt?"

"No," was the quick response. "I just know that it belonged to a Placerville family who brought it in, but I'm sorry I don't know who actually made it."

Placerville is an old mining town in California. It was known as Hangtown during its gold-rush mining days and I was hoping that we could relate the quilt to some early California pioneer family or to the colorful history of Placerville itself. But the vendor knew nothing more. Packing up our quilt, we headed home intent on learning more about our find. We knew there was going to be an antique appraisal fair in just a few weeks in our own hometown of Folsom, another historic California town with a well-known history museum.

Arriving home in high spirits, we carefully examined my birthday present. It was assembled from sixteen blocks, each block measuring 20 × 20 inches. The total quilt size was 80 × 80 inches. The foundation fabric was off-white cotton muslin with a quilt back of muted sage green with a dusty pink floral pattern, very similar to three other crazy quilt backings, vintage 1890–1900, that I had just seen exhibited at the Folsom History Museum's recent Antique Quilt Show.

The quilt was constructed without batting, top and back hand tied together with cotton thread at three-and-one-half-inch intervals and a border of hand stitched one-half-inch brown cotton edging. The materials included velvet, some crushed or cut and some solid and assorted striped, as well as damask, taffeta, silk, silk brocade, sateen, satin, velveteen, moire, and some men's ties. Ribbons (grosgrain, satin, and velvet), beaded fringe, flocked leaf and embossed velvet flower appliqués, and some crocheted flowers embellished the pieces. Many variations of feather stitching were used as well as other fancy embroidery stitches: straight, cretan, herringbone, and buttonhole. And on the bottom right corner of the quilt front was a faded blue denim patch in an odd, almost rectangular shape with a point at one end and the name "Robert" embroidered on it.

We could hardly wait for the appraisal fair because a quilt expert would be there and we were anxious to learn the age of our find, as well as anything else the expert would be able to tell us about it. The day finally arrived and we waited anxiously in line while three women in white cotton gloves unfolded, touched, pondered, and talked to each other about each of the quilts being presented ahead of us, concluding each time with a very careful and agonizingly slow refolding of each one.

Finally, it was our turn. In each of the appraisals before us, two of the women appeared to defer to the third and it was the third who slowly unfolded our quilt. She was not positive but she thought it was a turn-of-the-century quilt. One of the judges thought it might be later because she thought one of the patches was possibly too new to be turn-of-the-century fabric.

The primary quilt expert was examining the patches closely. Then she pointed to the denim patch with the embroidered name. "This is called a 'coffin patch' as it is shaped like a coffin," she said. "It means that the person died."

Behind that patch, sewn onto the backing on the other side, I had noticed a small piece of old fabric, about one inch by two inches in size and faded about as much as the backing itself. I pointed this out to her and said, "I think this is covering a hole in the backing."

This caused the expert holding that part of the quilt to look more closely. She fingered the small patch and suddenly stopped. "Wait," she said. "It feels like something is inside—some paper!"

There was a lot of noise and commotion all around us from the other appraisals taking place in the large museum room. But our little group suddenly became quiet as we looked at each other excitedly, our mouths open in surprise. Silently, the five of us waited as she worked out a few old stitches and slowly pulled out a piece of faded notebook paper folded carefully into a small, one-inch square. She handed it to me. I opened it and we read this handwritten inked note:

"This quilt was made in 1894 and 1895 by Elma Berry when she was 17 and 18 years old for Robert Cromwell."

Although the embroidery in the quilt was not as spectacular as that on the ones that had similar backings hanging in the previous museum show, that note and the provenance it provided made that crazy quilt much more exciting. The young age of the seamstress accounted for her less-experienced embroidery stitches and the mystery of who Robert might be added a new dimension to the quilt that none of us had anticipated.

We all speculated. Was Robert her fiancé and did he die before they could marry? Was she sewing a marriage quilt or a gift for him?

Excited by this incredible find, my daughter and I decided to trace the Cromwell and Berry families. We followed them from Placerville to Grass Valley, California, to Pike County, Illinois, and then to Ohio, Virginia, Kentucky, and finally to Hagerstown in Washington County, Maryland. By a strange coincidence, that is the same county my grandfather and his family and immigrant ancestor came from! Ultimately, our research showed us that the young seamstress, Elma Berry, did eventually marry a Cromwell, but a Dr. John Cromwell, and they had three sons. Their youngest was named Robert.

BETTY WILL *is a retired psychologist and artist who lives with her husband, Richard, a lawyer in Folsom, California. She loves to write and to make art quilts, crazy quilts, and yo-yo quilts as well as to collect crazy quilts. She is also a genealogist and recently had an article published about her mother's family in the Allegany County, Maryland, Genealogical Society's* Old Pike Post. *She is working on a book that is a ten-generation genealogical history of the same family.*

GRANDMA'S LACES

– – – – –

DELORES ENGELKEN

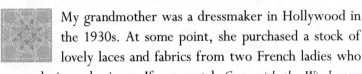 My grandmother was a dressmaker in Hollywood in the 1930s. At some point, she purchased a stock of lovely laces and fabrics from two French ladies who were closing a business. If you watch *Gone with the Wind* very carefully, you'll see some of those laces on the costumes.

When Grandma passed away, my Aunt Jill inherited this treasure trove because she was the only one in the family who was interested in sewing at the time. Over the years, she let me experiment with some of the laces and then passed them to me on her death. I can't begin to count the hours I've spent sorting through this incredible collection and planning how to use each delicate piece. I've appliquéd some of them to dresses, blouses, and pillowcases. I've even been known to glue a small piece or two to my golf hats. Everyone knows of my love affair with Grandma's laces.

One day, it finally occurred to me that I could see the laces every day if they were part of a bedspread. Even though I'd sewed and stitched for many years, I'd never quilted. But I didn't think it would be that hard to incorporate some of Grandma's laces into a bed covering.

I started by carefully hand stitching selected pieces onto alternating squares of ivory and ecru backings because the laces vary in shade from off-white to gray. That turned out to be the easy part.

I went in search of finishing advice and when it was suggested that I quilt around each lace piece, I almost went into shock. How could I possibly sew all those tiny stitches? But I was committed and the lace demanded the most elegant exposure.

It took a while but I eventually learned to use a quilting needle instead of a "horse-sized" one, how to make templates, and, most important, how to be patient. I laid the backing, batting, and quilt top on my patio floor then got on my hands and knees to baste it. I carefully tucked in the edges and hand stitched the front and back together, without binding. I made my own templates for the quilting pattern I wanted to use on the project's outer borders, and although I was panic-stricken at the thought of marking the fabric, I managed to pencil in my design.

As I finished the last quilting stitches, I thought how nice it would be to put a delicate lace trim around the edge. It would have been the perfect finishing touch but I didn't have anything in Grandma's collection that could be used that way. Wouldn't you know, that same day I received a package from my mother that included an old piece of cardboard wrapped with a few yards of fine lace trim. Mom wrote that it was Grandma's and did I want it? I'm sure my heart beat a little faster as I measured to see if it was enough. It was—just!

While making that quilt, I found a wonderful and supportive quilting group to join and am still a member of the Largo Cracker Quilters. In fact, my quilt hung in the guild's quilt show that year and even though my stitches were large and uneven and it didn't lay flat in some places, it won the Viewer's Choice award. We still use it on our bed every day even though some of the lace is a now a bit tattered and some pieces have completely fallen apart. But that doesn't matter, because I can see Grandma's laces every day.

DELORES ENGELKEN *and her husband, Dan, are enjoying retirement and an active life in Seminole, Florida. Attending weekly meetings with fellow Largo Cracker Quilter members is one of the highlights of her life.*

PINWHEELS

- - - - -

KENDRA HALL

In 1998, in spite of many reassurances from my surgeon to the contrary, the results of my biopsy came back positive. I had breast cancer. Following a mastectomy, I was sent to an oncologist for chemotherapy. But before he started the treatments, he shocked me by recommending a stem cell transplant because it was the best guarantee that the cancer would not return.

I had never heard of this form of bone marrow transplant but quickly turned to every available source of information to find out more about it. I was not reassured. Indeed, the thought of being isolated in a hospital room for three to six weeks triggered every claustrophobic fear I'd ever had. Even a visit to the hospital where the transplant would take place did not alleviate my apprehensions very much. I made them promise me that my room would have a window with a view.

When I told my quilting group about my prognosis and treatment, they immediately got to work to provide some comfort for me, though I did not know it at the time. Lots of half-square triangles were pieced and brought to our guild meeting to be signed. I was present at this meeting because I was still undergoing preliminary chemo and blithely signed one of the blocks, thinking it was for our outgoing president.

I underwent the transplant and received a great deal of comfort from the constant presence of my husband and the many e-mails and snail-mail messages from my friends. The surgery was successful and I was released from the hospital in less than three weeks to spend the next month in isolation in my home.

When I returned to my quilting group two months later, I was presented with a small quilt made of the signed half-squares which had been turned into colorful, scrappy pinwheel blocks. This quilt sat on my bed as I recovered so that I could easily read the messages written on it. Without fail, every time I read the signatures, a smile came to my face.

In addition to all the blocks signed by my friends in the group, the quilt assembler included the one block I had signed and every time I look at it, I laugh out loud. To me, it's become symbolic of the power of joining good wishes for ourselves with the loving wishes of others.

KENDRA HALL *lives with her husband, John, in Orem, Utah. They are the parents of three grown children and the grandparents of eight. Kendra has been actively involved in the Utah Valley Quilt Guild, serving as newsletter editor for thirteen years. She has taught quilting classes for the Utah Quilt Guild's Quilt Festival and, in 2005, chaired its Quilters for the Cure fund-raising campaign to raise money to fight breast cancer.*

FIRST DAY OF SCHOOL

– – – –

JOELLYN QUINN

 My first visit to our state guild's quilt show was with a new quilting friend. We were excited to be there, because we were going to have an opportunity to participate in an all-day quilt workshop. Of course, we wanted to get to the classroom early so we could get a good spot and be all set up and organized when class began. My friend set the alarm and we settled in for a good night's sleep, our machines and class supplies lined up by the door, all ready to go.

Fast forward to 6:30 A.M. The alarm sounds, showers are taken, makeup is applied, and we're dressed and ready for a big day. Off we went, machines in tow, across the walkway from the hotel to the convention center. As we looked out over the main street, we could see all the cars on their way to work, and I commented how dark it was out at this time of the morning. Oh well, must be a gloomy day.

We proceeded down the elevator and as the doors opened in the convention center, we were greeted by a night watchman. He looked at us and our machines a little funny, and then said the area was going to be closed for a couple more hours. By the time he got around to telling us that it wasn't even 6:00 A.M. yet, we were laughing so hard we could barely manipulate all of our bags back into the elevator.

Thinking we would at least have time for a nice leisurely breakfast, we found we were truly up before everyone because the restaurant wouldn't open for another thirty minutes. So we trudged back to our rooms for an early morning nap. Still laughing as we returned to the show for the second time that day, we agreed no one need know about our extra-early morning adventure but us and the security guard. That's when the elevator doors opened for us a second time that day and we were greeted by a guild volunteer who asked if we were the ladies who had been there before 6:00 A.M.

Moral of the story, ask for a hotel wake-up call!

JOELLYN QUINN *is a machine quilter, quilt artist, and teacher in the Madison, Wisconsin, area. She grew up the daughter of a professional seamstress and fell asleep many nights to the sound of a sewing machine. Having sewn clothing for many years herself, she found her love of sewing migrated to quilting when she made a quilt for her first grandchild— learning quickly that, unlike clothing, quilts "always fit."*

ROW ROBIN

- - - - -

MICHELLE BARROWES

It's a common feeling among quilters that we're all nice people with similar skill levels and good taste. But the truth is, quilters run the full gamut of good to not-so-good and everything in between as I learned when I participated in my first—and last—row robin with ten women I met online. Each one of us was to start a quilt with a single row of blocks. Then once a month, we'd send our package on to the next person in line so that they could sew the next row. At the end of all of this, each one of us was supposed to end up with enough rows to complete a quilt top.

I met some wonderfully talented quilters in the group but it quickly became apparent that some of the participants had very dubious taste in fabrics. For example, the quilt that started out with a patriotic theme got a row of dotted Swiss polyester blend that had been somewhat scorched in the ironing. A quilt of neutral colors such as beige, brown, and black got a row of pinwheels done in camouflage fabric. Some ladies deviated wildly from the original themes of the quilts as they made the rounds. One that started out with roses and pastels became trout and trees as rows were added. We saw a lot of polyester blends, which are not really suitable for quilting, and some fabric so thin, you could see through it. And then there were these garish combinations of colors and patterns that defied explanation.

It also became obvious that some of the participants were

new to sewing. I could certainly understand if the points of some blocks didn't match perfectly but some weren't even close. Lumpy, puffy squares that weren't square were common. One poor woman had so much difficulty maintaining a quarter-inch seam, she had to use iron-on patches on the back of her blocks to shore up her stitching. As I looked at them, I wondered how anyone was supposed to quilt through that.

Very few of the rows came out the same length as the original row, which meant that finishing up the quilts was going to be quite a challenge. One lady ignored the 48- to 60-inch length requirement entirely and started her quilt off with a row that was 104 inches long.

As we neared the end of this group project, we discovered that one woman was hoarding three packages. When the row robin organizer inquired about them, the woman was sketchy on the details but insisted she'd mailed them. But she hadn't. After the hoarder ignored our organizer's repeated e-mails and phone calls, the rest of us were asked to try making contact. So we all wrote, saying things like, "We understand things happen. It's okay. Just send your packages on to the next person in line."

She never answered us. I've since discovered that this is not uncommon with round robins and I've heard lots of horror stories about missing (stolen?) quilts. Most people who'd had a similar experience suggested that we file fraud charges against our hoarder and contact the local police, but when we warned her that we would do this, she made no response.

Finally, as most of us were getting our final packages in the mail, I searched online and discovered that the hoarder's husband had a prominent and somewhat public job with a major company. I e-mailed him the entire story of our round robin and told him that his wife was holding three of them back. I never heard from him directly but four days later, all the missing packages—the same ones that had supposedly been sent before—turned up at their intended destinations. Then our hoarder topped off her performance by sending a scathing e-mail to the row robin's organizer, blaming all the trouble on her.

I'm working on my round robin quilt now. I had to set aside some parts, and am doing a lot of re-sewing and reworking but it will be a lovely quilt when I am finished. It will be full of memories of all the rows I saw and sewed and of new friends that I now cherish.

MICHELLE BARROWES *lives with her husband and two college-age children in Greenville, South Carolina. She has a psychotherapy practice and enjoys sewing, crocheting, and painting in her spare time.*

SEWING GENES

- - - - -

ALLYSON BREHM

 The gentle whir of the sewing machine fills the air.

"I love that sound," my aunt announces. "It reminds me of Mom."

I am sewing a quilt square on a sewing machine that once belonged to my grandmother. It's an old black Singer that Grandma bought used and even though it's over forty years old, it's still in perfect working order.

My original plan had been to sew the square by hand as part of a project for a women's studies course in order to experience quiltmaking as many women had in the past. Unfortunately, my hand stitches are more like basting stitches and I can't see them lasting ten minutes let alone a hundred years! So I looked for another possibility and while visiting my aunt, I was delighted to find my grandmother's machine.

The quilt square I am working on will be pieced together with a collection of twenty other squares, each one made by a woman in my class. We have been studying women's fiber art traditions and plan to cap the semester with our own fiber art project. My square is a variation of a Nine Patch and I keep rearranging the pieces to make the colors look right. Greens, yellows, blues, and purples mingle together in a pile beside the sewing machine. As I stitch a yellow and blue triangle together to build a square, I remember my first sewing lesson.

I've been fascinated by sewing machines ever since I was

young and I was always asking my mom to teach me how to sew. She tried but she wasn't much better than the child she was teaching. So I turned to a neighbor, exchanging babysitting for sewing lessons. I made clothes for a long time—a dress to wear to an aunt's wedding, a Halloween costume, and lots of skirts. But I yearned to make a quilt. I've spent every one of the winter months in my life huddled under piles of quilts to stay warm. I feel a connection to fabric just like a woodworker feels a connection to wood. To me, the possibility of taking different pieces of fabric and pulling them together into one quilt that tells a story is mind blowing.

At the sewing machine, I place a small green square between the two blue and yellow squares to complete the first row of my Nine Patch. The Nine Patch is a traditional patchwork pattern and can be made very easily from scrap fabrics. I've always been drawn to patchwork-style or scrap quilts because their possibilities are endless.

There's a huge floor-to-ceiling cabinet in the corner of my parents' living room. Here, folded with great care so that you can see only bits of their patterns, lie the stacks of quilts that my mother has acquired. Some she started herself but left off in the middle, her ideas better than what her hands could create. Others are handmade from scraps of fabric and passed down through generations of my family. Still others have tags on them because they were bought in the bedding department of the local home-goods store.

Many years ago when I was in search of inspiration for my first quilt, I took a pile of the oldest quilts out of the cabinet in order to examine them further. As I held one of the oldest in my hands, I could feel the energy of my great-grandmother, my mother's grandmother, in it. The pattern was a traditional Log Cabin with lengths of light and dark fabric. No two pieces were the same. I flipped the quilt over to see the back and spent minutes running my hands over the stitching. I followed the sometimes curving stitches and thought about how long it must have taken her and how dedicated she must have been to the project. Tracing each sway with my fingers, I imagine Great-Grandma being lulled into quietness and thinking of something other than the task at hand. Or maybe she was a member of a quilting bee because hand quilting a large project like the one I held that day would be too much work for one person. So it could be that she gathered her friends together for the camaraderie of a quilting bee.

I bring myself back to the present as I introduce a cloudy purple fabric to the second row of my three-row square. It will be the center of the Nine Patch. Quilting is a centering activity and I'm grateful for the sewing genes that I've inherited.

In my family, we have two incredible needlewomen and one incredible needleman. My grandmother Audrey, whose machine I'm using, made clothes for her daughters and herself. A wool skirt that she once made for my mother now hangs in my closet and I love the thought of her taking time to make one of my most treasured possessions. I know that my grandmother Yetta, on my father's side, learned to sew where she grew up in Russia. At the age of nine, her parents sent her to work as a seamstress and she often worked a sixteen-hour day. She migrated to the United States in 1907 and continued to work as a seamstress. Her husband, my grandfather Samuel, came to this country just a few years before that and worked as a tailor in New York. After he married Yetta, they owned a tailor shop in Brooklyn.

I pick up the pieces for the final row of my Nine Patch. It mirrors the first. The middle section is different so the two ends act like bookends. This juxtaposition reflects my life because my ability to take pieces of cloth and turn them into something is a talent neither one of my parents have. The sewing genes skipped their generation. I am at home with a sewing machine and see endless possibilities in the never-ending rows of fabric at the store. My parents look lost when confronted by needle and thread. When I work at my parents' house, my father often comments how happy his parents would be to know that I sew.

Now the final stitches are complete. I remove the Nine Patch square from the machine to admire it. As I clip the dangling pieces of thread, my aunt returns to the room from the kitchen and looks over my shoulder before sitting down at the table.

"I used to love sitting and watching my mother sew," she tells me as she sips tea. "This is a special square because you are using your grandmother's machine."

I smile. She is right.

ALLYSON BREHM *has been a writer as long as she can remember. A trained journalist, she now works doing marketing and communications for nonprofit organizations. She resides in New Hampshire, where she stays warm in the winter wrapped in one of her quilts.*

WEEKLY SEWING CLASS

- - - - -

JACQUIE CAMPBELL

I once lived in a rural town in what is called the Alaska bush. We were located four hundred miles west of Anchorage and could be reached only by air though in the summer river barges could bring in large things like prefabricated houses and vehicles. We had a population of between five and seven thousand, depending on the season. Our town of Bethel was the hub for fifty-five other, smaller villages in a native Yu'pik Eskimo region. The villagers usually do not have running water or electricity in their homes. There is nothing that we would call economic development there so things such as sewing machines, quilt books, and fabric are hard to come by.

Bethel has the country's only prematernal home. This is where all the ladies from the villages and some from in town go to await the arrival of their bundles of joy. When I first moved to town, I stopped in to see what a prematernal home was and decided it would be a great place to volunteer because they had sewing machines, craft supplies, yarn, etc. It's a large facility and can house up to thirty-five women at a time. In the early spring, you can hardly move in there.

One day in late summer, I showed up to give my weekly sewing class and was surprised to see a new expectant mother. Though hardly a woman—she was only twelve years old and due in a month—she was from one of the native villages and quite

shy and reserved. In my experience, natives like to observe before they participate so I wasn't surprised when she decided just
to sit and watch.

That day, I was explaining how to make a Nine Patch from
strips and scraps using templates and a rotary cutter. The young
lady kept watching but looked sadder as the day went on. I asked
if she would like to join us but she said no, her village did not
have a sewing machine, so why learn?

At that moment, a light went off in my head—back to basics.
I learned how to sew by hand first, so why not teach these women
how to sew by hand as well?

The next day, I went back with needle and thread and asked
to see the young lady. I asked if she would like to make something for her baby and she said yes but not on the machine. So I
had her pick out the fabric she liked, showed her how to press it,
and then we set out to make a template from a cereal box like
my granny used to. That night, I left her to cut out the pieces
she'd traced with pencil on the fabric and the next day, I showed
her how to start sewing by hand. She took to it very well and I'm
sure she'd seen something similar because the natives sew all
their skins and furs by hand in their villages.

The next week, when I went back for my usual class, I was
surprised to see the young woman there. When I asked if anyone
had finished their "blankets," she jumped right up to show me
hers.

It was wonderful, a thirty-six-inch square of Nine Patch and
solid squares, complete with border, lined with flannel, backed
with cotton, and tied all over. I was in tears. It was so simple and so
lovely. And then she said to me, "Now I have something to give my
baby just like the other moms do."

I asked how she knew how to finish her quilt that way. She
told me that in her dream, she remembered seeing women at her

grandmother's house doing this to blankets. I was just amazed—
and ever since, I've been teaching the basics of "blanket"-making
the good ole fashioned way.

JACQUIE CAMPBELL *was born in Texas but spent her teen years in
Long Beach, Mississippi, where her parents still live in spite of Hurricane
Katrina. She now lives in Oklahoma with her husband, Shane, and three
children. Her mother and grandmother taught her to quilt the "old way,"
by cutting templates from a box of Kellogg's Frosted Flakes. Now she does
most of her piecing by machine but will still, for sanity's sake, do some
hand piecing from time to time. She enjoys sharing the art of quilting with
others.*

GETTING PINNED

－ － － －

HELEN GILMAN

I've always made quilts as wedding gifts for my children as they marry. My youngest daughter, Lydia, was living in Canada at the time of her wedding, which meant, of course, that I needed to go through customs with my present. When I got to the border, I was asked the usual questions including, "Why are you coming to Canada?"

"For my daughter's wedding," I said and a big grin spread over the custom agent's face.

"Oh, then you have a gift," he said. And my heart sank as I wondered what amount I would be assessed for a handmade quilt.

But I owned up and told him, "I always make quilts for my children when they get married."

"Oh, that's okay," he said and waved me through. I later found out that homemade items are not assessed.

After I crossed the border, my first stop was the home of my daughter's future in-laws. As I was showing them the quilt, we realized I had left some pins in it. Then we saw fleas! My cat loves to sleep on my sewing and knitting projects and I knew he had a bad case of fleas that summer but I hadn't realized that they'd taken up residence in my gift. As we took it outside to shake off the fleas and take out the pins, I shook my head over the unintentional additions to my gift.

According to my children, this was not the first time I'd left pins in a gift. In fact, my daughter-in-law Julie tells me that I not only left pins in their wedding quilt, I left pins in all four of the baby quilts I'd made for them as well.

You'll be happy to know that I've since switched to pins with small colored heads in hopes that I will see them before I give my quilts away.

HELEN GILMAN *is a native of the Lincoln/Woodstock area of New Hampshire. She started quilting while her six children were growing up. Education is important to Helen, and so at an age that's a bit older than the traditional college student, Helen attended the College for Lifelong Learning in New Hampshire and earned her Bachelor of Science degree in 1995.*

A QUILTING MEMORY

– – – –

ORA GREGORY

My dad always used to tell us, "My mother made quilts out of necessity and they were ugly but they kept you warm." And then he continued, "But your mother had a good sense of color so her quilts were good to look at as well as good to keep you warm."

After my mother passed away, my sisters and I met in the old upstairs bedroom where we all once slept. With Dad's help, we changed the room into a quilting studio.

As we gathered together with bated breath, we wondered what we would find. We started going through her fabric, boxes and boxes of fabric, pulling out UFOs (unfinished objects), sample blocks, started quilts, patterns. You name it, it was there.

With many an "ah," "ooh," and exclamations of "I wonder where this came from," we sorted everything into piles, remembering many fabrics from our past. Some scraps were left over from curtains, aprons, couch covers, or garments made for the family. "Look, I had a dress from this," one sister would say while another would spy another piece of fabric and say, "Oh, I had an apron from that."

We washed. We ironed. We laid out fabric and designed. Then we sewed, sewed, and sewed. In between times, we cried, laughed, and remembered our past.

We started by finishing up a Noah's Ark top and then a clown top—one for my daughter and one for a niece. There were several

FOR ESMERELDA, WITH LOVE

- - - - -

PAT GASKA

It had to be perfect, perfect color, design, and workmanship. I've been fortunate to see many perfect quilts over the years, admiring them and marveling at the talent of their makers. If others could achieve perfection, I hoped that I could too. After all, nothing less would do for my second grandchild.

Before she was born, I called her Esmerelda, a truly beautiful name, and I chose the New York Beauty pattern for *Esmerelda's Quilt*. It's a challenging pattern in four-and-a-half-inch blocks with curved seams and many points. Machine piecing would be possible, I thought, if I pinned carefully and sewed with great precision. But the results fell far short of perfection. The block simply wouldn't lie flat.

I redrafted the pattern and tried again. It wasn't quite right but I joined the first four blocks anyway, thinking that with adequate quilting it would be fine. After all, I've let go of perfection before, in quilting as well as other areas of life.

But after studying the joined blocks, I knew that they wouldn't do either. So I created yet another set of templates, this time for hand piecing. *Esmerelda's Quilt* would take much longer but the results would be worth the time invested.

The blocks went together perfectly and the quilt grew, slowly, each additional section being just what I had hoped for. The clear, lovely colors of the rainbow radiated from its center to

Sunbonnet Sue blocks that we pulled together for my nephew's baby. One of the great-grandchildren, a boy named Charlie, had reached the age of six without ever getting a quilt from his great-grandma. So we found a UFO of used material about the same age as Charlie and asked his mother if she would like us to finish it up as a quilt for him. She did, so we did, and later heard that "Charlie doesn't let anyone touch his quilt from his great-grandmother."

Eventually, we made quilts or pillows for every one of Mom's living descendents—including her twenty-five grandchildren and sixteen great-grandchildren—from the stash she left behind. We made crazy quilts, stripes, rails, whatever would fit the fabric at hand. And did we have fun? Yes, yes, yes.

ORA GREGORY *lives in the California foothills and is a member of th' Foothill Quilters Guild in Auburn. She has quilted off and on all of h' life, making quilts for others. When she's not quilting, Ora likes to crafts, collect salt and pepper shakers as well as nativity sets, and travel land, sea, and air. She also teaches Sunday school to the four-year-old her church and goes to Curves to stay spry and healthy.*

the edges, the hand stitches were tiny and even. It was close to perfect.

Thirty years earlier, when I began a quilt for Esmerelda's mother, Kati, it wasn't perfect so I gave up. It was years before I finished a different quilt for her, after learning all the rules of proper piecing and quilting. The quilt I made for Kati and Jody's wedding, made much later and with more experience, was better still.

I thought about why this small quilt needed to be so close to perfect. Perhaps it's because I wanted this new life to be perfect, too. I hoped that this little child would have health and abundant happiness. I hoped that she would look at the world and be amazed by its beauty. I hoped that she would always have people in her life to love and care for her—perfectly. But I knew there would be bumps in the road, tears and sorrows, disappointment and danger. At some point, she would discover that life is not perfect.

Chloe Kathleen Maier, my "Esmerelda," was born on December 23, 2003, and her quilt has comforted her every day since then. I'm sure she's never examined it for the size of its stitches, the neatness of its binding, or the choice of color. But perhaps one day she will. And perhaps one day, when she's older, Chloe will pull her baby quilt from its storage place and remember there was a grandma who wanted to give her only the absolute best.

PAT GASKA *is a quiltmaker, quilting teacher, and a member of two guilds—the Pine Tree Quilter's Guild and Wisconsin Quilters. She is the author of* Visual Illusion Quilts *(Dover Publications). She and her family, including grandchildren Teagan and Chloe, live in central Wisconsin. Semiretirement, after eighteen years of parish ministry, provides almost enough time to make all the quilts she would like to.*

QUILT PHANATIC

- - - -

ANNETTE MAHON

As a quilter and novelist, there's nothing I enjoy more than including a quilt or quilts in one of my stories. For years, while I was writing my romance novels, I thought about how I could combine sleuthing with a quilt group. I envisioned older women quilting together and solving murders over the quilt frame—sort of *Murder She Wrote* at the quilting bee. But my first attempt at a story didn't seem to gel and I finally put it aside.

One of my volunteer activities is ushering at the local venue for traveling Broadway shows. Driving home from a matinee performance, I was suddenly inspired. What if the actor playing the Phantom in *The Phantom of the Opera* was murdered while the show was playing at Gammage Auditorium? What if the actor was originally from Scottsdale and the lead character in my book, Maggie Browne, knew him? In fact, what if he'd grown up with her boys and was practically like another son to her?

I was off and running and the story flowed. I decided early on that I definitely wanted to include a pattern in my quilting mystery. Lots of mysteries were coming out with recipes, so I informally polled members at a couple of my quilting clubs and discovered that everyone loved the idea of a pattern in the back of the book.

Quilts flowed naturally into my story. The St. Rose Quilting Bee I created met every weekday morning as part of a senior guild at a Catholic church in Scottsdale. I set them in a mission-style church so that the women could sometimes quilt outside under the spreading branches of an olive tree. They hear the news of the actor's death while working on one of their group quilts, one of many for an annual fund-raising auction.

As the story developed, I decided that my women would make a memory quilt for the victim's mother. Since he was in the touring company of *Phantom*, Maggie organizes a BBQ at her family's ranch and invites all the company members. The bee women provide the quilt squares and pens so the actors can sign them. For the quilt block, I described a simple autograph block, a variation of a Rail Fence pattern with three strips of fabric, two prints on either side of a white or off-white strip that serves as the space for the autograph.

I sold my book, *A Phantom Death,* in January of 2000, at just the time *The Phantom of the Opera* was passing through Tempe again. Let me say right here that I am definitely a "phanatic" when it comes to this musical. I love it. When it plays in Tempe, I usher as often as I can.

For me, the play's timing was perfect. I'd just sold a book that included an autographed quilt. The quilt in the book was signed by the actors in the production of *The Phantom of the Opera,* the very same play that was on its way to my neighborhood. Inspired, I made up a stack of autograph blocks and took them with me to the theater. For several nights, I hung out at the stage door to collect autographs.

The actors were friendly and seemed to get a kick out of signing my blocks. One woman told me it was a first for her. Another said her grandmother made quilts and she thought it exciting that I was doing one.

At home, I worked on a center block, creating one that included an appliqué mask, a three-dimensional rosebud, and the embroidered words THE PHANTOM OF THE OPERA. I sewed the top together during the run of the show and took it with me during the show's final week to try and collect the last few signatures. I also took a photo of it and gave it to the house manager at the theater to post on the cast bulletin board.

I hand quilted the center appliquéd square, then machine stitched the rest of the top—mostly in the ditch. The quilt is black-and-white with red accents, and was quite popular at signings for my book *A Phantom Death*. I even had a hopeful attendee ask if it was a door prize. But I couldn't part with it. My *Phantom* quilt hangs on the wall of my sewing room, right next to my collection of *Phantom* music boxes.

ANNETTE MAHON *is a writer and quilter currently residing in Arizona, where she specializes in Hawaiian quilting. Her romance novels are all set in her native Hawaii while her mysteries take place in Scottsdale, Arizona. Visit her Web site at www.annettemahon.com.*

THE TREASURE CHEST

- - - -

R. C. DAVIES

When it comes to telling tales about quilting, there's no opening line more mundane than "I learned to quilt from my grandmother." Nevertheless, that's how my story starts. But there's something you should know about that first quilting lesson. My grandmother Marie Gaito died when I was barely five, way before I held a needle or wielded a pair of scissors. Yet she taught me how to quilt.

I thought that might catch your interest.

To this day, and I'm well past the point of freaking out over seeing my first gray hair, I still don't know very much about Grandma. She was born in Italy just before the first big world war and she had to stretch hard to make five feet tall.

I like to imagine Grandma Gaito when she was young and beautiful and curvy with dark hair. I like to think about how she defied her family to jump a ship for America with her only child, my mother, under her arm. I like to believe that my real grandfather was her one true love and not the man she was forced to marry. But that's just what I like to imagine. This is what I know.

After her boat docked in New York, Grandma eventually wandered to the Bronx to set up shop as a dressmaker. Mom says Grandma knew the bodies of the women in her neighborhood better than their husbands did. She'd watch customers trundle past her window while she stitched and say things like: "It's going to take five and a half yards of black cloth to cover that woman

when her husband finally dies," or "I'll be letting Mrs. Ro-
bichard's brown dress out soon. Babies make her so big so fast."

According to my mother, Grandma Gaito approved of the
man who was my father from the moment she met him. Dad was
a captain in the navy during the second big war, a tall handsome
guy with a mouth made for grinning. He and Mom got married
just before the navy sent him halfway around the world to some
place no bigger than a footprint. Grandma made the wedding
dress, of course, four yards of creamy satin cut slim and trimmed
with flowers embroidered with silver thread from a spool she'd
been hoarding for years.

Dad made it through the war, came home, got Mom pregnant, and then died when a truck hit him on his way to work.
Grandma made sure Mom bought a house with his life insurance
money and paced the floor at the hospital in his place the night I
was born. But then she passed away in her sleep before my fifth
birthday. After that, my mom's juices dried up. I remember trying to make her laugh when I was little but it was like working
the last bit of paste from a toothpaste tube—tough going with
little reward.

We had a nice house, probably the nicest on the block, but inside it looked like it was always waiting for people to start living
in it. Our dining room table was a bunch of boxes pushed together and covered with a cloth. The couch and chairs in the living room stayed right where the moving men dropped them
until I got big enough to rearrange them. It wasn't that Mom
didn't like our house. I just think she didn't notice anything—or
anybody—much.

She got a job at the post office when I started school and hired
old Mrs. Johnson to watch me in the afternoons until she got home.
Mrs. Johnson needed a lot of naps in the afternoons, "saving en-

ergy" she called it, so with nobody to play with, I started rummaging through the boxes in the house to keep myself amused. A lot of what I found was Grandma's or Dad's stuff—a shaving kit, a black lace scarf, ties, a box of books, and a stack of recipes written in Italian. I hid some of what I found in my room, figuring it might make Mom sad to see it. But other stuff—pots, pans, glasses, towels—I put where we could use them. If Mom noticed, she didn't say anything.

I saved the boxes that made the dining room table for last because I didn't know what we were going to eat on when I emptied them. When I finally got to those boxes, I had to be careful not to make any noise when I opened them, because Mrs. Johnson was right in the next room, the latest *Photoplay* magazine spread across her face to keep out the light. The first box was small but wonderful inside, filled with all sorts of baby clothes, including this christening dress with smocking from shoulder to shoulder, pearl buttons, and delicate yellowed lace around the bottom. I spent hours turning everything inside out to run my fingers over the hand-stitched seams. The next box held letters written on crackly paper with strange stamps on the envelopes. I couldn't read the writing because it was all curlicues and loops but I loved to look at it. The third box kept me entertained for a month. I'd wait each afternoon to hear Mrs. Johnson's regular breathing come from under the magazine then I'd pull it out and look at the pictures inside, running my fingers over the faces set forever in time, making believe that the mustachioed men and dark-eyed women were my family. Maybe they were.

I kept putting off opening the last box because I didn't know what I would do to amuse myself after that. But finally, after I'd thumbed through the pictures a second and third time, I eased the top off my last treasure chest. A little cloud of lavender scent rose up and then I saw Grandma Gaito's dark red pincushion, bristling with all sorts of needles and dangling threads. But that was nothing compared to what else I found.

At this point in my quilting life, I've conquered all sorts of patterns from Fool's Puzzle and Broken Saucers to something truly awful called Pigs in Space. So I can appreciate Grandma's simple choice for the quilt she never finished. She'd cut hundreds of small triangles for rows of Flying Geese and she must have culled them from every article of clothing she ever touched. I remember that day so clearly—Mrs. Johnson's soft snoring, the quivering light of the fading afternoon, my rapture as I carefully opened dozens of packages wrapped in light blue paper to reveal their lovingly collected contents. There were swatches of purple brocade the color of grapes, emerald silk embossed with twisting ivy, pieces of a black and red tartan that I can't imagine anyone ever wearing, blue taffeta to match a peacock's feathers, and a large swath of uncut sunflower satin that I drew slowly over my bare arms again and again just to enjoy its touch. That's probably why I never knew Mom was there until she called my name. I turned from my seat on the floor just in time to see her slumped in the doorway, her hand to her mouth.

"What are you doing?"

I turned away, frightened by her pale face. Only then did I look at the package I'd just opened, one of the last. It held nine larger pieces of fabric, three of navy blue, six of creamy satin embroidered with flowers in silver thread. I gingerly touched them with my finger then turned back to my mother. "They're Grandma Gaito's . . . and she wants me to have them."

"Oh no, no, not this." She lunged at me, snatching at the fabric as she came. I shrieked, waking Mrs. Johnson, who waddled in with newsprint smudged on her nose. She started fussing at

me while I screamed at my mother, and we carried on like that
for what seemed like forever. It finally stopped when Mom saw
the pieces of navy blue and satin cloth. She turned dead white
and dropped to her knees, clutching them to her face. I looked at
Mrs. Johnson, who only shrugged. "I gotta go," she said. "John
will be waiting on his supper."

I thought Mom had stopped breathing, but then she started
making these funny sounds like a coughing bark and I finally realized she was crying. I'd never seen her cry before and it scared
me half to death. But I wanted that fabric. "They're Grandma
Gaito's," I repeated shakily. "And she wants me to have them."

Mom didn't move for a very long time. I kept watch on her
while I rewrapped my treasures and put them back in the box.
Finally, she looked up and her face was all squashed with big wet
places under her eyes. She watched me pick up the fabric scraps
for a while and then finally said, "I don't know how to sew."

"That's all right," I told her as I put the pincushion back on top
of the fabric. "Grandma Gaito does. I'm going to learn from
her."

At the time, I sounded a lot more sure of myself than I really
felt. But you know, having those samples of Grandma's work to
study and touch probably did more for me than any book or class.
Mom never did pick up a needle and thread but she did make sure
that I had lots of fabrics to play with. Sometimes, she'd even join
in when I'd lay the scraps out on our new kitchen table to see
how the colors and patterns could go together.

I sewed and practiced a lot before I finally felt like I could
make a quilt with the fabric that Grandma left behind. My first
project was a pillow for my mother made from some of the navy
blue wool and cream satin. She kept it on her bed until the day
she died and asked that it be buried with her. And that's what
I did.

R. C. DAVIES *is now a grandmother, and she's making sure all of her grandchildren know how to sew. A retired English teacher, she lives in the Hill Country of Texas near Austin, and enjoys long walks with her dogs when the bluebonnets are in bloom.*

CLIMB THE MOUNTAINS

- - - - -

DORI GALTON

In Jewish weddings, it is traditional for the bride and groom to stand under a chuppah, a canopy or cloth, held above their heads. The chuppah symbolizes the home the couple is about to build and share together, open on all sides, welcoming family and friends to join as witnesses to the joyful occasion. The chuppah is usually made of cloth and oftentimes is a prayer shawl.

For my daughter Shala's wedding, we decided to make a small quilt for the chuppah and we asked friends and relatives of the bride and groom to contribute squares. Since I am a quilter, I took on the responsibility of organizing the collection of the squares and of sewing them together into a quilt. The first step was to cut and send out squares of muslin to all those who had indicated that they would like to contribute. It was left entirely open-ended as to how the square-makers could create and decorate their squares—they could be drawn, pieced, embroidered, or whatever their imagination and creativity suggested.

The wedding was scheduled for August and I must have sent out the blank squares early in the spring, requesting that they be returned to me by the end of May so that I would have plenty of time to arrange the squares, to cut out sashing and borders to frame them, to sew the whole together, and to have it quilted and ready to be attached to poles, which would be held up over the wedding couple during the marriage ceremony.

The variety of squares that were returned to me was a wonderful reflection of the interests of the bridal couple, Shala and Warren, and of the skills, imagination, and ingenuity of their friends. Their friends did not adhere to typical gender roles and, in fact, some of their male friends were especially creative. One knit his square in fanciful patterns and colors of wool, presenting me with the challenge of making it fit and stretch into the six-inch squares of the others. Another made a colorful pieced square in tans and burnt orange. A college friend created a cartoon of the bridal couple under the chuppah out of bits of yarn, partly embroidered, partly tacked with thread into a design. Warren's friend Will, who had introduced the couple and was the realtor who found them their home, made a fabric collage of their Seattle craftsman-style house. My husband had his square of muslin Xeroxed with two photographs of the bride and groom as children, wearing coincidentally similar striped shirts and with surprisingly identical preadolescent toothy grins. He wrote on it with fabric pen, "Stripes and teeth form a new union!"

Many of the squares were personalized to mirror something unique about Shala and Warren's relationship. Since the couple met while cross-country skiing and they continue to enjoy camping and hiking together, several of the squares featured colorfully embroidered couples sitting around a campfire or with skis standing guard outside a ski hut. Shala's sister embroidered a saying of John Muir's, "Climb the mountains and get their good tidings. Nature's peace will flow into you as sunshine flows into trees. The winds will blow their own freshness into you, and the storms their energy, while cares will drop off like autumn leaves."

One of the squares was a fabric painting, showing the bridal couple in a Chagall-like scene, floating on skis above the Seattle Space Needle. I embroidered a copy of their wedding invitation, including the potato-print image of a dancing couple and the wording of their invitation, which invited family and friends to "Come dance with us at our wedding." For another square I made an embroidery showing the bride and groom under a chuppah, in which I used a bit of fabric left over from the first quilt I had ever sewn, which I'd made for Shala for her high school graduation. I cut the tiny black-and-white printed cotton, fashioning it into a miniature, matching appliquéd shirt and dress for the Shala and Warren look-alike bridal couple.

The deadline for the return of decorated squares came much too soon for some of the contributors. There were frantic last-minute phone calls and overnight mailings of some beautifully crafted and custom-designed squares. I took a lot of care, laying them out so they balanced and complemented each other in color and theme. There were some restraints. One family of four each made an embroidered square, which needed to be placed in a row since they had written out their tribute to the couple together. Finally, I sewed the squares together in between fabric sashing of regal blue and gold, which tied all of the different squares together into a glorious whole.

On a lovely Sunday afternoon, in a grassy glade at Mt. Rainer National Park, Shala's and Warren's siblings walked down the path holding the chuppah aloft on wooden poles. In front of the assembled wedding attendees, they formed a rectangle with the chuppah-quilt and its many colored squares, linking the two families. Shala and Warren walked in, beaming, arm in arm, and stood to be joined in marriage before family and friends under the chuppah that many in attendance had contributed to with love and care.

Now, almost four years later, the quilt hangs in a prized spot on the landing of Shala and Warren's home in Seattle, and Maya, their two-year-old daughter, loves to be lifted up so she can look at and touch the beautiful hanging. She wants to hear the story of the squares and feel the different textures of cotton, wool, shiny antique buttons, and pearls that her parents' families and friends used to adorn the marriage chuppah. It continues to be a reminder of their beautiful wedding day and the love that others contributed to their union.

DORI GALTON *lives with her husband, John, on Laughing River Farm alongside the Connecticut River in Vermont. She thinks that the "real" quilters are like the women from Gee's Bend, Alabama, who salvage bits of fabric from their loved ones' overalls and sew them into beautiful and useful coverlets. While Dori also quilts for her loved ones, she thinks of her quilting as a real luxury: buying gorgeous dyed cottons, cutting them into tiny pieces, and stitching them back together into colorful patterns.*

STRANGE OPPORTUNITIES

- - - - -

JUDY LAQUIDARA

One spring morning, I read a story in the paper about a fairly young mother of four children, pregnant with her fifth child, who had died. The paper listed the church she attended. It happened to be the same church attended by the woman who cuts my hair, so when I saw Robin at my next appointment I asked her about this lady. She told me it was really sad. The young mother homeschooled her three school-age children, she got sick, there were complications, and she just died— something fairly simple that affected her heart, as I recall.

A few months later, I was at the dentist with my son for a checkup. Our dentist is always so busy and it takes forever to get an appointment. Chad had a cavity and I was trying to make an appointment for him after school when they told me they had a cancellation for "tomorrow." I hesitated—who wants to go to the dentist two days in a row?—but went ahead because it probably would have been a six-month wait for another appointment.

So it was back to the dentist the next afternoon. We walked in and there was an older lady sitting there with three children, not really old but enough so that I doubted the children with her were hers. Somehow, I just knew those children belonged to the young mother who had died. I don't know how I knew it but I did.

The dental assistant came out and called for Anna. The lady tending the children said that Anna would be coming with her dad, and one of the other children took her place. Then Dad came in with Anna, a lively four-year-old.

I was working on binding a quilt while waiting for Chad. Anna walked over and commented on my work and her dad said something like, "Mom would like that. She loved quilts."

Anna said, "Oh, Dad, you know Mom is far, far away in heaven!"

My heart sank. The next day, I called the dentist and inquired to make sure I was absolutely right. Yes, those were the children whose mom had died. I said I wanted to make quilts for the kids but I wanted to drop them at the dentist office because I wanted to do it anonymously. They agreed to help me.

Well, I'm nosey so I went back to find the young mother's obituary in the newspaper archives online. And when I read it, I got a chill right down my spine. The mom's maiden name—her full name, first, middle, and last—was exactly the same as the first, middle, and last of my maiden name—Judy Lynn Miller! How weird is that?

Think I was at the dentist office two days in a row for a reason?

JUDY LAQUIDARA *lives in Owensboro, Kentucky, with her husband and son. She is a long arm quilter, quilt designer, and quilt teacher.*

QUILT THERAPY

- - - - -

JEANINE WILLIAMS

I discovered quilting at the same time I was struggling with the decision to end my twenty-year marriage. My self-esteem was very low, my future was cloudy, and I just didn't know where my life was going. At the time, I could never have predicted how important quilting would become as I worked through my personal struggles.

I had found this local quilt shop and decided to take a class to learn how to make a simple quilt. I enjoyed it so much, I started looking around for patterns and began making some easy, strip-pieced quilts on my own. Then I read in one of the books I was using about making quilts for charity. That sounded like a great project to do with other people so I asked around my church to see if anyone wanted to join me in making quilts for the local social services Christmas store.

There were seven of us who met that first time. Together, we made nine quilts for the store and had so much fun, we decided to meet monthly and became Quilts from Cornerstone, a ministry of Cornerstone Baptist Church. Currently, we have twenty dedicated women who meet once a month.

This quilt group gave me something positive to latch onto when my life could have easily turned to the negative. The more I struggled with my deteriorating marriage and the depression it caused, the more energy I poured into this quilt ministry. This work and the group helped me survive a divorce, my children leaving home, loneliness, a job layoff, a long unemployment, dating, and eventually, a remarriage. In fact, it was the quilt ministry that attracted my new husband to me and to my true heart.

Throughout the years in this group, I've seen women struggle with divorce, cancer, the deaths of loved ones, moving across the country, and just everyday stresses. We have learned that when we are hurting, the best way to heal is to reach out to others. And through it all, we've made some beautiful quilts.

JEANINE WILLIAMS *has been quilting for about eight years and has a passion for making quilts to donate to various local charities. In 1998, she founded a quilt ministry named Quilts from Cornerstone. For more information, you can visit its Web site at www.cornerstone4u.org. Jeanine lives in Council Bluffs, Iowa.*

QUILT-OLOGY

- - - -

GAEL ZWIEP

I've been a middle school teacher for nearly twenty years now. While I don't believe it's a job require- ment, I do know our principal has a bias toward hiring quilters. Nancy keeps this wall hanging over her desk—in the Schoolhouse pattern, what else—and takes note of applicants who notice it and those who don't. That's why, out of a faculty of twenty-seven, we always have a good handful of stitchers. Nancy claims that she likes to hire quilters because they're used to see- ing impossible projects through to the end—and that's just the quality you need to teach sixth, seventh, and eighth graders.

Of course, where you have quilters, you eventually get a quil- ters' gathering. Our group started informally when a couple of us sat down at the lunch table with sandwiches, spools of thread, and pincushions. At the time, I was just learning to appliqué and I was bent over a deep green square of cotton to which I was sewing a pansy-shaped bit of lavender. The eighth-grade math teacher, Melissa, sat down to embroider details on a small stack of Sunbonnet Sue blocks. We were both newbie teachers that year and we bonded as soon as we shared our first smile.

If you've ever been a member of a quilt group of any kind, you understand how one thing leads to another. For example, when Nancy's husband left her for a new life with someone he met in an online chat room, we extended our informal lunchtime quilt gatherings to full evenings of "stitching and bitching." We parsed out advice on dating and men when she recovered enough to consider accepting a dinner invitation. And then we talked her out of taking that lame-excuse-for-a-husband back when the online cutie didn't work out the way he planned.

We average seven women when we get together to share potluck, sewing, and socializing. Over the years, we've helped one another through a wedding fraught with family politics (that was Melissa), the birth of twins (that was me), finding a house, dealing with an ornery neighbor, and just the general frustrations of working with students who are experiencing the first flush of hormones.

About two years ago, Nancy was rattling on about this man she'd just met while we lingered over pasta and wine. He was funny, liked her dog, shared her love of the outdoors, and claimed to be familiar with the on-switch of a vacuum cleaner.

"Sounds like a Nine Patch man," Melissa said. "I'd keep him."

"A Nine Patch man?" Nancy asked. "What do you mean?"

Melissa looked a little embarrassed but explained: "Some people are like quilt patterns to me. A Nine Patch person is easy to get along with, just like the pattern. A Log Cabinite is someone who's full of ideas, each one bigger than the last. You know what I mean?"

We all sat there with our jaws hanging open a little, staring at her.

"How long have you been doing this?" I asked.

"Almost since I started quilting. Some patterns are quick and easy to use while others make you pay attention to lots of little details, just like people." She looked around the table. "You think I'm nuts, don't you?"

"Nuts?" Nancy crowed. "Not at all. I think you just invented Quilt-ology."

"Quilt-ology?"

"Sure, think about it. We've got astrology, numerology, graphology, and phrenology—all ways to try to understand people's personalities, right?" Nancy asked. We all nodded. "So why not Quilt-ology?"

We had some more wine, each of us sunk deep in thought, and then we began to talk. While it may not be scientific, we all agreed that you could use Quilt-ology as shorthand for describing certain personality types.

Ever since that initial revelation, our little group has settled on some quilt patterns that we use to cover the basics of human character. Of course, as any good quilter knows, it's the way you use color and combine patterns that makes all the difference between something you're proud to keep on your bed and an unfinished bit of business that you hide in the dark of your closet.

So here are our top choices. I'd be willing to bet that before you get to the end of this list, you'll have thought of several other block patterns that really fit some of the people you know.

Nine Patchers: In quilting, a Nine Patch is just what it says—nine squares of fabric sewed in three rows of three. This is the workhorse of quilting, the block pattern that most beginners start with. Like a pair of black pants, a Nine Patch goes with just about anything.

Nine Patchers are just like the pattern for which they are named—good to have around, you can never have too many of them. They are flexible, adaptable, and easy to get along with. By themselves, they tend to be overlooked. But when you get a whole bunch of Nine Patchers together, you just know that everything will work out just fine.

Log Cabinites: When you make a traditional Log Cabin block, you start in the center and add pieces one at a time, each one bigger than the one before. Half of the pieces will be of dark fabric, the other half light. Once you've made a number of Log

Cabin blocks, you can turn them and lay them out in a variety of ways to make different color patterns.

In Quilt-ology, a Log Cabinite is someone who's not completely trustworthy, because they're so easily influenced by their surroundings. It must be a Law of the Invisible Universe that every group of people must include a Log Cabinite. You know the type, the guy you meet at a party who tells story after story, each one outstripping the last. Log Cabinites have been known to use up all the oxygen in a room, leaving Nine Patchers feeling overwhelmed.

Drunkard's Pathers (D-Pers for short): When a quilter is ready to sew something other than a straight line, she will often tackle the curving Drunkard's Path. The result can either be an eye-popping quilt or a fancy pile of scrap.

Like the pattern, D-Pers can be either magnificent or impossible, depending on the way they're cut from the beginning. Life with a D-Per is sure to be interesting but they need firm guidance in order to amount to much. In other words, they're needy. If D-Pers don't get templates to live by, their future holds nothing but scrap.

Cathedral Windows (CW-ites): In this day of rotary cutters and sewing machines that come with attachments that can do anything except baste your Thanksgiving turkey, sometimes a quilter just wants to slow everything down and keep it simple. A bed covering made in the Cathedral Windows pattern requires nothing— no batting, no quilting—except patience to hand sew the muslin frames and then fold them back to reveal unexpected splashes of color and excitement inside.

A CW-ite is that quiet person sitting in the corner of a busy room who doesn't look so much shy as self-possessed. CW-ites are worth the time it takes to get to know them because they're interesting and they have depths that a casual acquaintance will never discover. I served on a board with a CW-ite once. She'd always sit there quietly, listening to the conversation swirling around her. Then just when it seemed like the whole committee was becoming a muddle, she'd ask just the right question or make the right comment to get us on track again.

Grandma's Flower Garden (GFG): Have you ever seen a honeycomb? You know, all those six-sided cells, one right next to the other with dozens upon dozens of winged workers busy filling them up? That's the Grandma's Flower Garden pattern, hundreds of hexagons in different colors sewed to one another in all sorts of patterns.

To brag for just a moment, the GFG is my original contribution to Quilt-ology. When we started talking about personality types, I immediately thought of this pattern and how much my paternal grandmother fit its profile—always busy, versatile, down-to-earth, and able to do six things at once equally well. A GFG is a natural organizer, the type of woman who knits when she sits, and never says no if there's volunteering to be done.

Okay, that's our list. I know it's short but it will get you started. So, what kind of person would you say fits Broken Dishes or Tumbling Blocks or Sunbonnet Sue?

GAEL ZWIEP *teaches, quilts, and happily shares her life with her husband, twin sons, and three dogs in the Berkshire Mountains of western Massachusetts. She admits to a genetic predisposition to being a GFG. When she's not slashing fabric with a rotary cutter, you'll find her in the garden, reading a good book, organizing a church supper, or raising money to stock her local food pantry.*

YOU KNOW YOU'RE A QUILTER IF . . .

A Collection of Quilting Truisms

- - - -

GATHERED FROM A VARIETY OF SOURCES

You know you're a quilter if . . .
Your grandchildren check the collar of your blouse for pins
before they let you take them anywhere.

You know you're a quilter if . . .
You've worn a thimble to bed.

You know you're a quilter if . . .
You didn't notice you'd worn a thimble to bed.

You know you're a quilter if . . .
The phrase "fat quarter sale" makes you drool.

You know you're a quilter if . . .
You have more fabric in your house than the local quilt shop.

You know you're a quilter if . . .
You get home from a trip, get your pictures developed, and find
you have more photos of floor patterns and wallpaper patterns
than you do of the mountains or sea.

You know you're a quilter if . . .
You don't think there's anything strange about keeping UFOs
in your closet.

You know you're a quilter if . . .
Your coworkers pick threads from your clothes
without comment.

You know you're a quilter if . . .
All the charges on your credit card are from quilt shops.

You know you're a quilter if . . .
You have a credit card just for quilt shops.

You know you're a quilter if . . .
You have a scrapbook full of fabric swatches.

You know you're a quilter if . . .
Your closet is full of fabric draped over hangers while your clothes have to make do with the floor.

You know you're a quilter if . . .
You've driven through the worst snowstorm of the winter in order to get to a quilt guild meeting—and there are thirty other women there who did the same thing.

You know you're a quilter if . . .
You group the clothes in your closet by color.

You know you're a quilter if . . .
You have a pincushion in every room of the house.

You know you're a quilter if . . .
You understand that "continuous bias" has nothing to do with race relations and everything to do with cutting, marking, and folding fabric.

You know you're a quilter if . . .
You don't believe that rayon is a fabric.

You know you're a quilter if . . .
You've brought your sewing machine on a business trip.

You know you're a quilter if . . .
You really do like or really don't like paper piecing.

You know you're a quilter if . . .
You've never used freezer paper in your freezer.

You know you're a quilter if . . .
You don't like to iron but you do like to press.

You know you're a quilter if . . .
You still get a thrill when you think about the time you sewed
your first curved seam.

You know you're a quilter if . . .
You can't balance your bank statement but you can calculate in
your head the total yardage needed to complete a queen-sized
Lone Star quilt.

You know you're a quilter if . . .
You've quilted to stay sane.

You know you're a quilter if . . .
You've quilted so you won't go crazy.

You know you're a quilter if . . .
Your husband understands when you tell him you're going out
to strip with friends.

GLOSSARY OF QUILTING TERMS

- - - - -

Generally speaking, most people use the words "patchwork" and "quilt" interchangeably to mean bed coverings that are warm to sleep under at night and are made by sewing pieces of fabric together in a pattern that is pleasing to the eye. But to quilters, these two words don't necessarily belong together. A quilt may be patchwork—or it may not. And conversely, a bed covering made of patchwork may be a quilt—or it may not.

Here's a quick guide to many of the terms you'll find in the stories in *American Patchwork* so we don't lose anyone along the way.

appliqué: This is a process of sewing small pieces of fabric onto a larger background piece of fabric. It allows for great flexibility of design and fine details. Appliqué is generally considered an advanced quilting technique but its origins are in the humble patch applied to a garment to cover a hole.

backing: Also referred to as the bottom layer of a quilt, it is the third of the three-part quilt sandwich: top, batting, backing. In a quilt, the backing is usually quite plain in comparison to the top.

batik: High-quality Indonesian cotton or silk that is dyed using a wax-resist method. A design is drawn on the fabric with melted wax and then it is immersed in dye. The areas covered with wax resist the dye and become the pattern in the cloth. Batiks are prized for the high quality of their cloth, their vibrant patterns, and intense colors.

batting: This is the fiber used in the inside of a quilt. It is what gives the quilt its warmth. Nowadays, batting is made of polyester, cotton, or wool. Quilters commonly refer to the piece of batting used in a quilt as "the batt."

binding: These are narrow pieces of straight-grain or bias-cut fabric that are sewed around the outside of a quilt to hide its batting and the unfinished edges of the top and bottom.

blocks: This is the basic design unit of a quilt with a pieced top. When a quilter chooses a patchwork pattern, it will be repeated in blocks over the length and width of the quilt top.

border: This is fabric sewed around the outer edges of the quilt pattern. Visually, it serves as a frame around the fanciest part of a quilt. A border can be a solid piece of fabric or it can be pieced.

comforter: Technically speaking, bed coverings that have a top, backing, and batting that are tied together are comforters, not quilts. But generically, most people refer to both tied bed coverings and quilted bed coverings as quilts. Often the batting in a comforter is thicker than in a quilt. Historically, comforters have also been called "comforts," "comfortables," and in parts of Pennsylvania, "haps."

crazy quilts: In recent years, quilters have devised several methods for using a rotary cutter to make quilt tops out of irregularly shaped pieces of fabric. Traditionally, however, crazy quilts start with a piece of backing fabric, often unbleached muslin, to which patches of other fabrics are hand stitched to form an irregular pattern. Crazy quilting began during the Victorian era, was quite a fad at that time, and is still very popular today. Once a crazy quilt block is complete, it is often embellished with all sorts of fancy embroidery, appliqué, beads, and buttons.

fat quarter: Small pieces of fabric measuring approximately 18 × 22 inches. They are sold separately or in themed or color-coordinated groups at quilt shops, quilt shows, and fabric stores. Because they are smaller, fat quarters are easier to work with than larger pieces of fabric and many patchwork patterns lend themselves to this size with a minimum of waste.

hand quilting: The process of sewing the three parts of a quilt sandwich together by hand. At its most basic, this stitching is meant to hold the batting in place, but if that was quilting's only purpose, straight seams would suffice. As anyone who's ever examined a quilt closely will testify, quilting is used to create patterns with thread and needle that enhance the patterns established by the fabric used in a quilt top.

Log Cabin: One of the oldest known patterns in patchwork, the Log Cabin begins with a center block—traditionally red to represent the hearth in a real log cabin—and then narrow strips (logs) are sewed successively around the center. No one's quite sure where this pattern was first used but it appeared in the United States around the time of the Civil War.

long arm (or longarm) sewing machine: A relatively expensive piece of equipment, the long arm sewing machine extends the area where fabric can move under the machine itself. This adaptation of the traditional sewing machine makes all types of plain and fancy machine quilting possible. Many people with long arm machines provide commercial quilting services.

Nine Patch: This is arguably the oldest known patchwork pattern. It is just what it says, nine square pieces of fabric joined to one another in three rows of three. A Nine Patch is very versatile and is often the first block pattern that a quilter learns.

paper or foundation piecing: Usually used for patterns that benefit from precise sewing, pieces of fabric are cut to a pattern and then stitched in a certain order to paper or a foundation fabric. In paper piecing, the paper is removed when the block is finished. In foundation piecing, the foundation fabric becomes part of the quilt.

patch: An individual piece of fabric cut into a particular shape that will be joined with other patches to form patchwork.

patchwork: The overall pattern formed by the joining of patches to one another. The process of creating patchwork is called piecing.

quilt: Traditionally, a bed covering consisting of a fabric top and bottom with the space between filled by batting. The three layers are then stitched together in a pattern across their length and width.

quilting: The process of machine or hand stitching the three layers of a quilt together. Quilt stitches most often follow a precise pattern meant to enhance the fabric and pattern choices made by the quilter.

rotary cutter: Arguably the most revolutionary tool to hit quilting since the sewing machine, a rotary cutter looks like a small pizza cutter; it has a very sharp, circular blade set in a handle. Used with a matt to keep the blade from marring a work surface, a quilter can cut through several layers of fabric at the same time with a rotary cutter and ruler so that patches are more uniform.

Scrappie quilt: A form of patchwork that uses many instead of a few different fabrics. A Scrappie quilt's intent is to allow a quilter to use up a lot of odds and ends of fabrics left over from previous projects.

stash: The hoard of fabric owned by an individual quilter. Most quilters will admit that they are addicted to fabric and often buy yardage for which they have no immediate use but just want to own. A quilter's stash is equivalent to a watercolorist's paint box.

stitch in a ditch: The simplest form of quilting, done by hand or by machine, which follows seam lines where blocks or patches are joined to one another.

tied comforter: A way of securing the top, bottom, and batting of a bed covering together without the necessity of stitching them. The ties, which can follow the fabric pattern of the quilt or not, are usually of wool yarn, perle cotton, or embroidery thread. This process is also called tufting.

COPYRIGHT ACKNOWLEDGMENTS

- - - - -